MARRIAGE BY THE BOOK

Book 8

Fanning the Flames of Romance

Biblical advice for
Individuals
Couples
Small groups
Sunday school classes

Doug Britton, MFT
Marriage and Family Counselor

LifeTree Books
Sacramento, California
www.LifeTreeBooks.com

ISBN 1-930153-08-2

Except when otherwise noted, all Scriptures are taken from
the HOLY BIBLE, NEW INTERNATIONAL VERSION.
Copyright 1973, 1978, 1984 International Bible Society.
Used by permission of Zondervan Bible Publishers.

P200520050120

Printed in the United States of America

LifeTree Books
Sacramento, California

I want to express my deep appreciation to my sons Zach and Josh, their wives Holly and Paige, and countless friends for their many invaluable suggestions.

I especially thank my brother Gordon for his tireless editing and proofreading. Most of all, I am deeply grateful to my wife Skeeter for her many hundreds of insightful comments, painstaking editing, prayers and love.

•

Now to him who is able to do immeasurably more than all we ask or imagine, according to his power that is at work within us, to him be glory in the church and in Christ Jesus throughout all generations, for ever and ever! Amen (Ephesians 3:20-21).

BOOKS BY DOUG BRITTON

Conquering Depression: A Journey Out of Darkness into God's Light
Defeating Temptation: Biblical Secrets to Self-Control
Getting Started: Taking New Steps in My Walk with Jesus.
Healing Life's Hurts: God's Solutions When Others Wound You
Overcoming Jealousy and Insecurity: Biblical Steps to Living without Fear
Self-Concept: Understanding Who You are in Christ
Strengthening Your Marriage: 12 Exercises for Married Couples
Successful Christian Parenting: Nurturing with Insight and Disciplining in Love
Victory Over Grumpiness, Irritation and Anger

Marriage by the Book (eight-book series)
1: Laying a Solid Foundation
2: Making Christ the Cornerstone
3: Encouraging Your Spouse
4: Extending Grace to Your Mate
5: Talking with Respect and Love
6: Improving Your Teamwork
7: Putting Money in its Place
8: Fanning the Flames of Romance
Marriage by the Book Group Leaders' Guide

To see a current list of books by Doug Britton,
visit www.DougBrittonBooks.com.

Contents

Preface

Sex seems so simple. The mechanics certainly are. But to join together, body and soul, in the sweet and thrilling sexual intimacy God intends for a married couple sometimes seems an impossible dream. Some common complaints:

- ✓ "The only time he talks is when he wants sex."

- ✓ "She pushes me away when I get romantic."

- ✓ "I feel like screaming when he touches me."

- ✓ "It's her duty to have sex with me."

- ✓ "You want me to do *what?!*"

If you've been frustrated with your sexual relationship, this book is for you. And it's for you if you have a wonderful friendship and sex life, but desire even greater intimacy.

Take a minute to think about where you got your ideas about sex. If you're like most of us, you learned about sex from television, movies, novels, magazines, pornography, secular teachers and sex manuals. Or the kid next door.

At first, many people find worldly ideas about sex exciting and appealing, but in the end, they are disappointed. The world promises freedom, but the result is slavery to depravity (2 Peter 2:19), emptiness and broken relationships.

In the Word of God, we read the Lord's instructions for a pure and exhilarating sexuality that can be experienced by a husband and wife. *Fanning the Flames of Romance* is based on these timeless truths, truths that help us escape the world's corrupting influences and enjoy a delightful sexual relationship.

In these pages, you will study the importance of a close friendship for a great sex life. You will see the difference between simply "having sex" and expressing and receiving love. And you will read about how to make love with love, playfulness, gusto and tenderness—just like Solomon and his beloved in the Song of Songs.

May God richly bless you and your marriage bed.

Doug Britton

Introduction

We live in an age of countless and ever-changing opinions and theories about marriage. When we seek guidance, it is hard to know whom to believe.

Yet there is a dependable source to which we can go, one proven trustworthy and constant throughout history—the Word of God.

 All Scripture is God-breathed and is useful for teaching, rebuking, correcting and training in righteousness, so that the man of God may be thoroughly equipped for every good work (2 Timothy 3:16-17).

The Bible covers it all, including communication, forgiveness, decision-making, finances and making love. God invented marriage. He knows how to make it work.

Fanning the Flames of Romance takes ageless truths from the Bible and helps you apply them in your marriage. It is the eighth in an eight-book series called *Marriage by the Book.* Although it stands as a complete book by itself, I encourage you to also read the other seven books, since they build on one another, each presenting the Bible's teaching on a different aspect of marriage. The eight books are:

(1) Laying a Solid Foundation

(2) Making Christ the Cornerstone

(3) Encouraging Your Spouse

(4) Extending Grace to Your Mate

(5) Talking with Respect and Love

(6) Improving Your Teamwork

(7) Putting Money in its Place

(8) Fanning the Flames of Romance

Each book is for individuals, couples and classes.

The books are designed to be studied by an individual, a couple, a small group or a church class. They also can be assigned as homework by a pastor, counselor or mentor. Although written for married people, these books also are excellent resources for those considering marriage.

Each book has six chapters, making it convenient for a six-week small group study program. The *Group Leaders' Guide for Marriage by the Book* shows how to set up and lead classes.

Each person should have his or her own book.

Numerous personal application questions (with spaces for answers) are scattered throughout this book. If you are studying as a couple, it would be best for each person to have a book. That way, both husband and wife can write answers and comments.

Names have been changed.

As you read, you will see that I have drawn upon the experiences of people I have counseled. The stories are true, but names and identifying details have been changed to maintain confidentiality.

Who is "Skeeter"?

If you have read some of my other books, you may remember that I sometimes referred to my wife as "Susan." In this book, I call her "Skeeter." Don't worry. Skeeter is Susan's nickname. I still am married to the same lively, intelligent, God-fearing woman.

Getting the Most from this Book

In *Laying a Solid Foundation,* the first book in this series, I wrote several guidelines to help you get the greatest possible benefit from studying. The following are some key points.

Examine your relationship with God.

Jesus declared, *"You must be born again"* (John 3:7) and added, *"I am the way and the truth and the life. No one comes to the Father except through me"* (John 14:6).

God created you and he loves you. Listen to Christ's invitation: *"Come to me, all you who are weary and burdened, and I will give you rest"* (Matthew 11:28). If you have not yet done so, I invite you to surrender your life to Christ by saying the following as a prayer:

> *"Dear Lord, I confess that I am a sinner. Please forgive my sins and accept me as your child. I invite you to be my Savior and the Lord of my life. I surrender myself to you in the name of Jesus Christ."*

If you prayed with sincerity, Christ accepted you into his Kingdom and you are now a Christian. Welcome to the family of God!

I accepted Jesus Christ as my Savior and Lord today. Thank you, Jesus!

_____   _____
Signature   Date

Not only will God help your marriage, he will transform your life. You have an exciting life ahead of you. These four suggestions will help you get started in your Christian walk:

- Tell someone that you accepted Christ.

- Read the Bible daily, starting with the Gospel of John in the New Testament.

- Join a Bible-believing church.

- Pray regularly.

Take the plank out of your own eye.

Most of us focus on our spouse's faults. Yet Jesus said, *"First take the plank out of your own eye" (Matthew 7:5).* As you read, focus on changes *you* should make, not on those you wish your spouse would make.

Write an answer to each question.

This book is designed to be interactive, with numerous "Personal Application" questions throughout to help you apply the material to your life. Think about each question and write your answer. In addition, underline key points as you read. Write notes in the margins or in a notebook.

If you find it difficult to write answers, I encourage you to overcome your reluctance or embarrassment. The more you involve yourself by answering the questions, the more the information will become part of you and the more you will change.

Study even if your spouse does not.

I hope you and your mate will study and learn together, but your spouse may refuse. In fact, he or she may say, "I don't have any problems. You're the one who needs help. Study by yourself."

What could be more frustrating? After all, your mate *does* have problems. Everyone does. You know it, and God knows it. But your spouse doesn't seem to know it.

However, even if your mate refuses to study, work through this book yourself. Don't say, "I'll read it, but only if you will." Instead, learn how to be the best husband or wife possible. God can perform miracles in your personal life and your marriage as *you* change.

Do not be overwhelmed by the information.

You may become discouraged by the many suggestions in this book, thinking you cannot follow them all. Don't feel condemned and do not try to do everything at once. There is a lot of material.

At the end of each chapter, "Putting It All Together" provides a place to identify one or two things you want to work on most. That should be enough for starters. Come back to the chapter later for fine-tuning.

Be appreciative if your spouse makes an effort.

Do not feel insulted if your mate follows some of the suggestions in these books. For example, if he or she asks you out to dinner, don't say, "You're just asking because you're supposed to." Or if your spouse apologizes for something, resist the temptation to respond, "You don't really mean it. You're only saying that because you know you're supposed to apologize."

The point of these books is to help people change. Be appreciative when your spouse makes an effort.

Do not give up when there are setbacks.

There is a pattern I see over and over: A couple experiences great improvements, then old problems reappear and one of them says, "I guess we haven't changed. I give up."

When this happens, don't give up. All marriages suffer reverses and difficult moments from time to time. Expect them, learn from them and press on.

Invite Your Mate to Study with You

I encourage you and your spouse to study this book together. Talking about these lessons can be exciting, even life-changing. Yet such discussions can degenerate into accusations, name-calling, anger and hurt feelings. The following guidelines will help you avoid common problems and get the most out of your time together.

Invite (but don't pressure) your mate.

Let your spouse know you would enjoy studying together, but don't start a fight over it. If your mate says "no," don't get into an argument. Instead, study alone.

Set up a regular time to talk.

Do not simply say, "We need to talk about this book sometime." Make specific plans. Agree on a schedule. For example, you could study together:

- Fifteen minutes every night after dinner or

- 7:00 to 7:30 p.m. Monday and Friday nights or

- 9:00 to 10:00 a.m. every Saturday.

Decide if you want to read separately before talking.

Some couples like to read a chapter separately and then get together to discuss it. Others prefer to read together and talk about the material as they go. Still others do both, reading when apart and then together.

Start with prayer.

Invite God to play a central part in your discussion. Ask him to:

- Show each of you what you need to work on the most.

- Give you grace and discipline to change.

- Help you talk with love and respect.

Read a few paragraphs, and then discuss them.

A common pattern for those who study together is for one person to read a few paragraphs out loud, after which both discuss the material. The second person then reads, followed again by a brief discussion. This process is often repeated for 20 or 30 minutes.

Don't worry if you find a point that is especially relevant and spend the entire time focusing on it. The idea is to deal with real issues, not just turn pages.

When you review the "Personal Application" questions, each can read his or her written answers or just share verbally.

Get involved.

Do not simply say, "I agree with that." Go into detail. Explain why you think what you do.

Share *personal* insights when you talk.

Talk about how the material applies to you, personally. Instead of pointing out what you think your mate should learn, discuss changes *you* should make.

Don' t get mad at your mate's comments.

If you tell each other your answers to "Personal Application" questions, you may sometimes be hurt by things your spouse says. Ask God to help you avoid reacting in anger or self-pity. There may be things you can learn from your mate's answers. Ask the Lord to help you respond with wisdom, understanding and love.

Write your own answer to each question.

Do not ask your mate to write answers for both of you. Write your own answers.

Ask before reading what your spouse wrote.

Your spouse may write thoughts, fears or temptations he or she desires to keep private. Agree not to read each other's answers without permission. As I wrote before, each person should have his or her own book if possible. Otherwise, think about writing your answers in separate notebooks to maintain privacy.

Personal Application

Talk with your spouse and then write the day(s) and time(s) you will discuss this book together.

Studying in a Group or Class

Some of the material in this book deals with sensitive issues. If you are studying in a group setting, I suggest you discuss chapters 1-2 in the full group and chapters 3-4 in separate groups of men and women. When studying chapters 5-6, review the key themes in the full group, then have couples move to separate areas for private discussions.

Chapter 1

Adopt God's View of Sex

I am my lover's and he is mine (Song of Songs 6:3).

God designed marriage to be the most intimate of human relationships, a wedding of body to body as well as soul to soul, a relationship surrounded by love. He intended sexual intimacy between a husband and wife to be pleasurable and fun for both. Through the ages that has not changed. He still wants our lovemaking to flow from an ongoing friendship and commitment to love for all of life.

Pure sexuality is different from worldly sexuality.

The pure, wonderful sexual relationship that God intends a husband and wife to enjoy and the sexuality we see in the world are vastly different from one another. The world sees sex as being about the same as scratching an itch. God's view is that sex provides a married man and woman a wonderful way to express and receive love.

Although the mechanics of holy sex and sinful sex may seem similar from the outside, the experience is profoundly different. This can be illustrated by considering fire. Fire is life-giving in some circumstances, yet in others, it is life threatening. If you were in the wilderness, you might welcome a campfire. You could stand near it to keep warm, and you could roast marshmallows over it. But if you were to encounter a forest fire, it would be an entirely different matter.

You would fear for your life. Sex, like fire, can be delightful or destructive.

 *Personal Application*

Write a prayer asking God to help you clearly see the difference between pure sexuality and worldly sexuality as you read this book.

The Bible's Message

In this chapter, we will take a look at the Bible to find out what God says about holy sex. As you will see, God describes the sexual relationship between husband and wife as something wonderful—something to be enjoyed, as well as his means of creating life.

If you find it difficult to read these verses because you have come to see sex as something unpleasant or wrong, don't despair. God has an entirely different type of sexual experience in mind for you than what you might have experienced in the past. He will help you substitute the pure for the impure.

Song of Songs

In God's big romantic poem, the Song of Songs (also known as the Song of Solomon), love between husband and wife is described in such sensuous terms that my mother's parents wouldn't let her read it as a child! The song uses images of gardens, coconut palms, wine, goats, lilies, spices and doves to describe a love that is *"as strong as death" (Song of Songs 8:6).*

The frankness and sensual imagery give a living picture of the joyful sexual relationship that God intends for marriage. As you read the following verses, notice that:

- The husband and wife are friends as well as lovers.

- Each person eagerly anticipates making love.

- Each desires to give the other pleasure.

- Each praises the other's beauty.

- Each talks about their sexual relationship without inhibition.

- Each thoroughly enjoys making love.

 Chapter 1. The woman speaks: *(2) Let him kiss me with the kisses of his mouth—for your love is more delightful than wine. (16) How handsome you are, my lover! Oh, how charming! And our bed is verdant.*

Man: *(15) How beautiful you are, my darling! Oh, how beautiful! Your eyes are doves.*

Chapter 2. Woman: *(3) Like an apple tree among the trees of the forest is my lover among the young men. I delight to sit in his shade, and his fruit is sweet to my taste. (4) He has taken me to the banquet hall, and his banner over me is love. (5) Strengthen me with raisins, refresh me with apples, for I am faint with love. (6) His left arm ["hand" in the King James, Revised Standard and Amplified Bibles] is under my head, and his right arm [or "hand"] embraces me. (16) My lover is mine and I am his; he browses among the lilies.*

Chapter 4. Man: *(1) How beautiful you are, my darling! Oh, how beautiful! Your eyes behind your veil are doves. Your hair is like a flock of goats descending from Mount Gilead. (3) Your lips are like a scarlet ribbon; your mouth is lovely. Your temples behind your veil are like the halves of a pomegranate. (5) Your two breasts are like two fawns, like twin fawns of a gazelle that browse among the lilies. (10) How delightful is your love, my sister, my bride! How much more pleasing is your love than wine, and the fragrance of your perfume than any spice! (11) Your lips drop sweetness as the honeycomb, my bride; milk and honey are under your tongue.*

Woman: *(16) Awake, north wind, and come, south wind! Blow on my garden, that its fragrance may spread abroad. Let my lover come into his garden and taste its choice fruits.*

Chapter 5. Woman: *(10) My lover is radiant and ruddy, outstanding among ten thousand. (11) His head is purest gold; his hair is wavy and black as a raven. (12) His eyes are like doves by the water streams, washed in milk, mounted like jewels. (13) His cheeks are like beds of spice yielding perfume. His lips are like lilies dripping with myrrh. (14) His arms are rods of gold set with chrysolite. His body is like polished ivory decorated with sapphires. (15) His legs are pillars of marble set on bases of pure gold. His appearance is like Lebanon, choice as its cedars. (16) His mouth is sweetness itself; he is altogether lovely. This is my lover, this is my friend, O daughters of Jerusalem.*

Chapter 6. Woman: *(2) My lover has gone down to his garden, to the beds of spices, to browse in the gardens and to gather lilies. (3) I am my lover's and he is mine; he browses among the lilies.*

Chapter 7. Man: *(1) How beautiful your sandaled feet, O prince's daughter! Your graceful legs ["joints of thy thighs" in the King James Bible; "curves of your hips" in the New American Standard Bible] are like jewels, the work of a craftsman's hands. (2) Your navel is a rounded goblet that never lacks blended wine. Your waist is a mound of wheat encircled by lilies. (3) Your breasts are like two fawns, twins of a gazelle. (4) Your neck is like an ivory tower. Your eyes are the pools of Heshbon by the gate of Bath Rabbim. Your nose is like the tower of Lebanon looking toward Damascus. (5) Your head crowns you like Mount Carmel. Your hair is like royal tapestry;*

the king is held captive by its tresses. (6) How beautiful you are and how pleasing, O love, with your delights! (7) Your stature is like that of the palm, and your breasts like clusters of fruit. (8) I said, "I will climb the palm tree; I will take hold of its fruit." May your breasts be like the clusters of the vine, the fragrance of your breath like apples, (9) and your mouth like the best wine.

Woman: *May the wine go straight to my lover, flowing gently over lips and teeth. (10) I belong to my lover, and his desire is for me.*

Chapter 8. Woman: *(3) His left arm [or "hand"] is under my head and his right arm [or "hand"] embraces me. (10) I am a wall, and my breasts are like towers. Thus I have become in his eyes like one bringing contentment. (14) Come away, my lover, and be like a gazelle or like a young stag on the spice-laden mountains.*

Genesis

In the Bible's first words about it, God defined marriage as a man and woman becoming "one flesh," making it the most intimate of human relationships.

The man said, "This is now bone of my bones and flesh of my flesh; she shall be called 'woman,' for she was taken out of man." For this reason a man will leave his father and mother and be united to his wife, and they will become one flesh (Genesis 2:23-24).

Proverbs

The book of Proverbs shows us that God intends our times of lovemaking to be exhilarating. In Chapter 5, the husband is encouraged to rejoice in his wife and enjoy her breasts.

 May your fountain be blessed, and may you rejoice in the wife of your youth. A loving doe, a graceful deer—may her breasts satisfy you always, may you ever be captivated by her love (Proverbs 5:18-19).

Some translations of the Bible use different words for "captivated." Re-read these verses, substituting the following words for "captivated": "ravished" (King James Bible); "transported with delight" (Amplified Bible); "exhilarated" (New American Standard Bible). The commentators in the New International Version Study Bible suggest an additional term: "intoxicated."

 *Personal Application*

Summarize what God is saying about sex in the above passages.

Write a prayer asking God to help you experience and enjoy pure sexuality with your spouse.

Think of something from your own lovemaking that makes you feel particularly close to your spouse and share it with him or her. For privacy's sake, feel free not to write it down here.

Examine Your Attitudes

Mark and Donna talked to me about difficulties in their sexual relationship. Mark said he was free and uninhibited. He was sure Donna's inhibitions were their only problem.

It was true that Donna felt uncomfortable about sex. However, after they talked, Mark was surprised to hear me say they *both* needed to change their attitudes. Donna saw sex as dirty or sinful. Mark, on the other hand, had developed what I call a "pornographic mentality" and was bringing worldly attitudes into the marriage. Sex for him was about *performance,* not giving and receiving love.

Mark and Donna illustrate two common ways people think about sex. One is to think of sexual intimacy as disgusting or impure. The other is to focus only on the physical part of sex, paying little attention to *loving* as an intimate friend.

Here are some ways distorted ideas about sexuality get started. Check each one that applies to you.

☐ **"My parents were distant."**

If your parents were cold and distant from one another, it may have made you uncomfortable about physical intimacy.

☐ **"One of my parents had an affair."**

If either parent had an affair, it probably had an impact on your thoughts and emotions.

☐ **"A relative told me sex is dirty or disgusting."**

Words you heard as a child can impact the way you look at sex. For example, when Sarah was a little girl, her aunt told her that the naked human male is the ugliest thing God ever created. Those words stuck in Sarah's mind and deeply affected the way she looked at her husband.

☐ **"I heard negative preaching about sex."**

If the preaching you heard about sex stressed the negative, it might have made you afraid of sexual intimacy.

☐ **"I was sexually abused or raped."**

It makes sense that a terrible sexual experience could impact your attitude about sex. This is discussed in Chapter 3.

❑   **"I got into pornography."**

Pornography is a dreadful way to learn about sex. Pornography presents sex simply as an instinctive drive, not as a way for husband and wife to express and receive love. You get weird, inaccurate ideas that you may try to live out in your own life—and then wonder why you fail, never realizing that you believed lies.

❑   **"My past sex sins distorted my attitudes."**

Chapter 4 offers ways to deal with past and current sexual sins, sins that have an impact on your sexual relations with your spouse.

❑   **"I accepted media pictures of sexuality."**

Our society presents untrue, ungodly pictures of morality and sexuality and calls these pictures normal and good. Take a movie, for example, that portrays two unmarried people about to have sex. The music builds to a crescendo. The photography is spectacular. Sin is made to appear fun or wonderful, even loving.

Everywhere we look, there are positive images of immoral sex. It's even used to motivate us to buy mouthwash and automobiles.

Even seemingly innocent entertainment, such as television sitcoms, pollutes our minds with impure ideas about sex. Watching actors portray sexual immorality and make jokes about illicit sex for hundreds of hours every year cannot help but affect you negatively.

I used to read detective books and espionage novels. But many years ago, the Lord prompted me to stop reading them, because the writers began to include unhealthy sex scenes. Many women have stopped reading certain women's magazines and romance novels for the same reason.

❑ "I believed my teachers."

Elementary school, high school and college classes are often sources of misinformation. Students in many high schools and colleges are encouraged to be sexually active and to be open to homosexuality.

 *Personal Application*

Have you had a negative or impure view of sexuality?
❑ Yes　❑ No

If so, list some sources of your negative attitudes (for example, "My parents never kissed or touched").

1.

2.

3.

Write a prayer asking God to free you from these influences.

Putting It All Together

Key point: Enjoy your sexual relationship. It is a gift from God.

•

Memory verse: *"I am my lover's and he is mine" (Song of Songs 6:3).*

 *Action Plan*

Choose one or two things from this chapter to work on this week.

1.

2.

Chapter 2
Cultivate Your Friendship

A friend loves at all times (Proverbs 17:17).

A friend of mine often says, "My wife is my best friend." He may not realize it, but by nurturing his friendship with his wife, he is almost certainly giving his sex life a boost. A husband and wife who are best friends most likely will have a wonderful sex life.

Most wives understand the importance of friendship to a satisfying sex life. But many husbands are like Larry, a man who came to me for marriage counseling. When he came home from work, Larry was either silent or critical toward his wife Julie throughout the evening. Then, when he went to bed, he wanted to make love. Julie became increasingly unresponsive and said she felt used. Larry felt rejected and bitter.

He didn't understand that most women only desire to make love when they feel loved. And he did not understand that men, as well as women, experience a *dramatically* greater degree of sexual intimacy when they have a deep and growing friendship.

Not all men are like Larry, of course. Many want to connect emotionally, not just "have sex." They want to be best friends with their wives.

What does it mean for a husband and wife to be each other's best friend? Friendship is, among other things, talking daily, taking time to understand one another, sharing jokes and sharing grief, comforting one another and inspiring each other to new heights. In this chapter, we will look at some ways to be better friends, knowing this will also make us better lovers.

 *Personal Application*

Do you and your spouse seem like close friends? Score yourselves from 0 to 10.

0	1	2	3	4	5	6	7	8	9	10
Not very close   Very close

List three specific reasons for your answer. When you are done, talk with your spouse and compare answers.

1.

2.

3.

Talk Together Often

If a husband and wife seldom speak, or speak only about superficial things, their friendship slowly fades away. They become roommates instead of soul mates.

This can happen in an established, happy marriage. Skeeter and I had been married for more than 20 years and had a close friendship when she went back to school to get a degree in landscape architecture. She carried a heavier than average load, and was so busy that for months we rarely spoke. One night, I looked at her sleeping by my side and realized she seemed like a stranger. When I told her this, she was shocked. We both rescheduled our lives to make time for each other.

A close relationship requires a pattern of daily conversation. What would God think if you only prayed to him once a year? Make it a habit to talk every day, especially at key times of the day, such as right after work or during dinner.

Sharpen your communication skills.

When you talk with your mate, talk about hopes and fears, successes and failures. Talk about your experiences with God. Share from your heart.

Also talk about fun things. Make plans together. Practice being a good listener. Look for ways to have fulfilling conversations.

The following guidelines will help you have good talks. Evaluate your communication patterns as you read them.

 *Personal Application*

Score yourself from 0 to 10 on each of the following statements. Then briefly identify any changes you need to make.

- "0" means, "I really need to work on this."
- "10" means, "I do great at this."

I talk about things that matter with my mate every day.
  My score (0-10): _____
  Needed changes:

I actively participate in conversations.
  My score (0-10): _____
  Needed changes:

I share ideas without giving speeches.
  My score (0-10): _____
  Needed changes:

I listen well without interrupting.
My score (0-10): _____
Needed changes:

I discuss difficult subjects without anger.
My score (0-10): _____
Needed changes:

Show Respect

Respect is another key ingredient in friendship. In the Song of Songs, both of the lovers see the other as special and unique. The husband even says his bride is perfect (Song of Songs 6:9).

Both husband and wife are to show respect.

 Honor one another above yourselves (Romans 12:10).

> *The wife must respect her husband (Ephesians 5:33).*

> *Husbands, in the same way be considerate as you live with your wives, and treat them with respect (1 Peter 3:7).*

Respecting your spouse means treating him or her as an equal. It means talking as to an adult, not as to a child. It means listening and treating what he or she says as important. It means avoiding sarcasm and cutting remarks. It means not insisting that your way is the only way.

 *Personal Application*

Rate yourself from 0 to 10 on each of the following statements. Then briefly identify any changes you need to make.

- "0" means, "I really need to work on this."
- "10" means, "I do great at this."

I speak respectfully.
  My score (0-10): ____
  Needed changes:

I talk to my spouse as to an adult, not a child.
   My score (0-10): _____
   Needed changes:

I enjoy knowing my spouse's opinions, even when they are different than mine.
   My score (0-10): _____
   Needed changes:

I only tease or joke in ways my spouse enjoys.
   My score (0-10): _____
   Needed changes:

I praise much more often than I criticize.
  My score (0-10): _____
  Needed changes:

_____

Be Romantic throughout the Day

Romance is too good a thing to only enjoy at night in the bedroom. Bring romance out of the bedroom and into your daily lives. As you go through the day, look for ways to show love. Tell your spouse he or she is cute, cuddly, good looking or strong.

Every day is full of opportunities for kissing, holding hands and hugging. Pass through the room where your husband is reading and gently kiss his ear. Walk through the garden where your wife is pulling weeds, take her hand and kiss it.

Men, be sensitive to *how* you hug. Many women say they hate being hugged because it means their husband wants immediate sex. Most wives crave, instead, a friendly touch. Practice non-sexual hugging.

Express words of love such as "I love you" and "You look beautiful today." Call from work to say, "I can't wait to be home with you." Every day, greet your spouse at the front door with a smile and a hug.

Wear clothes you know your spouse enjoys seeing you in. If you don't know what clothes to pick, ask your mate. Of course, when others are around, dress modestly.

The Bible says to *"serve one another in love" (Galatians 5:13).* Think of special ways to minister to your mate. Give gifts like flowers, candy, love notes, lingerie, perfume. Cook a favorite meal.

 The mandrakes send out their fragrance, and at our door is every delicacy, both new and old, that I have stored up for you, my lover (Song of Songs 7:13).

Since people are different, ask your spouse what he or she enjoys. Be creative, thoughtful and surprising.

 *Personal Application*

Do you need to be more romantic throughout the day?
❑ Yes ❑ No

Ask your spouse what things you do that make him or her feel loved. Write the answer here.

Write one to three things you will do to be romantic in the next two days.

Spend Special Time Together

Working or playing side-by-side gives you time to develop your friendship in a natural, easy way. Although it is good to do some things on your own, be sure to identify things to do together.

Enjoy shared activities.

Don't let life's problems drag you down. Have fun together. Talk with your mate to see if you share an interest in something you would like to do together. If you can't identify any shared interests, be adventurous and enter your mate's world. Join your spouse in some of his or her activities.

Use the following ideas to get yourselves thinking:

✓ Study the Bible together every morning.

✓ Work together in a ministry.

✓ Work in the garden together.

✓ Do crossword puzzles as a team.

✓ Learn a language together.

✓ Play together on a coed volleyball or baseball team.

✓ Collect something together, such as stamps or antique plates.

✓ Read a book together, with each person taking turns reading out loud.

 *Personal Application*

Talk with your spouse and then write at least one way that you will spend time together.

Go on dates frequently.

Going on dates is a wonderful way to improve your friendship. If you can afford to go to a restaurant from time to time, do it. You're not wasting money. In fact, some people think the most romantic words in the English language are "Let's go out for dinner." You are making a sound investment to strengthen your marriage.

Don't let a lack of funds hold you back. There are many ways you can have fun dates without spending money. Skeeter and I have had great times going for walks, reading to each other from favorite books, playing tennis and rollerblading.

Don't just say, "We should go on dates." Make a plan, perhaps setting aside one evening a week as a date night. If both of you want to go out, but neither wants to take the initiative to make plans, serve your spouse by being the one who organizes the date, carefully taking your mate's likes and dislikes into account.

 *Personal Application*

Write ideas for three dates that you would enjoy.

Talk with your spouse and then write a plan for your next date. Include a specific time that you will go out.

_____

Go on vacations together.

Go on short holidays and longer vacations with just the two of you—no kids, no friends. Having a longer stretch of time together, uninterrupted by, "Daddy, Bobby hit me!" or "Mommy, I'm supposed to bring the snacks to Cub Scouts tomorrow," can allow a couple to talk about what really matters and fan the flames of their romance. Even after the children are raised and gone, a couple can see each other with new eyes after a few stress-free days in a fresh location.

Come, my lover, let us go to the countryside, let us spend the night in the villages. Let us go early to the vineyards to see if the vines have budded, if their blossoms have opened, and if the pomegranates are in bloom—there I will give you my love (Song of Songs 7:11-12).

God likes the idea of a couple spending time together. After all, in the Old Testament he established something that sounds like a one-year honeymoon.

If a man has recently married, he must not be sent to war or have any other duty laid on him.

> *For one year he is to be free to stay at home and*
> *bring happiness to the wife he has married (Deu-*
> *teronomy 24:5).*

People sometimes make the mistake of waiting until they retire before going on vacations together. By waiting, they miss out on all the enjoyment and benefits of taking vacations in their earlier years. In addition, they run the risk of *never* spending this type of time together if one of them becomes physically incapacitated or dies.

"We can't afford to go anywhere."
Many couples say they would like to take a vacation, but they can't afford it. If you are creative, you can overcome this obstacle. Camping in a national forest can be very inexpensive. You don't need the latest equipment. In the early years of our marriage, Skeeter and I camped with little extra other than what we had around the house. Sometimes we even camped without a tent.

"We always visit relatives on our vacations."
Although it can be wonderful to spend time visiting family members, let me encourage you to also enjoy some holidays with your mate, alone.

"But we have children."
If you have children, most of your vacations should be for everyone together. However, it is good for Dad and Mom also to take some short holidays or vacations without the kids. Leave them with family members or friends. Return the favor another time by watching your friends' children.

A word of caution
Let me close this section with a warning. If a lot of tension has built up in your marriage, a vacation can be a

nightmare, unless you are prepared to spend time talking things through and praying.

About six years after we married, Skeeter and I went on our first vacation without the kids. We went backpacking in the Olympic Mountains in Washington State.

We thought we had been getting along fine as we went out the door, leaving our three small boys in the hands of a bachelor friend from the south (who, it turned out, fed them grits and candy bars).

But as we started hiking up the trail, we discovered that we weren't doing fine; several areas of tension had built up and we had some difficult conversations the first two or three days. We finally got through them and ended up having a trip that was both hard and fun.

 *Personal Application*

When was the last time you and your spouse went on a holiday or vacation together?

Where did you go?

Talk with your mate and make a plan to go on a holiday or vacation together. Write your plan here.

Make Your Spouse Your Best Friend

I have known many people who left their spouse and married someone else. Walt, a pastor, was typical. He seemed totally dedicated to the Lord, his wife and his family. Then one day he did something that shocked and deeply saddened everyone he knew—he left his wife and moved in with another woman.

How could this have happened? Walt started out "counseling" with the woman, a member of his church. As time went on, she found herself enjoying his kind personality, and he began to take pleasure in the way she responded to him.

An emotional bond grew as they spent time together and talked about increasingly personal things. Finally, they decided they had "fallen in love," so he left his wife and moved in with her. The results in Walt's life, her life and the lives of everyone else involved were tragic.

Learn a lesson from Walt and this woman—and the many other people who have made similar errors: Getting too close to someone of the opposite sex is dangerous.

Throw yourself into your marriage. *Never* allow someone to take your spouse's place in your life.

Here are some safeguards:

- Do something to strengthen your marriage every day.

- Be cautious about sharing intimate information with someone of the opposite sex.

- Do not flirt or play "innocent" games with others.

- Unless you are a pastor or counselor, do not develop a helping relationship with someone of the opposite sex unless your spouse is in agreement and involved.

- If you are a pastor or a counselor, be wise! Make and follow personal boundaries.

- If you wish you were married to someone else, pray to be free from this desire and to love your spouse more.

- Do not tell your mate how attractive, sensitive, wonderful or smart someone else is.

- Stay alert. If you begin to develop an unhealthy emotional (or physical) bond with someone, flee! Don't play games.

 *Personal Application*

Do you need to change the way you interact with others of the opposite sex? ❑ Yes ❑ No

If you checked "yes," what changes will you make?

Putting It All Together

Key point: Develop a close, ongoing friendship with your spouse.

•

Memory verse: *"A friend loves at all times"* *(Proverbs 17:17).*

 *Action Plan*

Choose one or two things from this chapter to work on this week.

1.

2.

Chapter 3

Let God Heal Your Wounds

He heals the brokenhearted and
binds up their wounds (Psalm 147:3).

Note from Doug: This chapter offers help to those who have been sexually abused or raped. If these pages do not apply to you, feel free to skip them and go to Chapter 4.

However, if your spouse or a friend has been abused or raped, you may want to keep reading to better understand what he or she went through.

Joan's father often told her, "Any girl who has sex before she gets married is like a piece of candy that is thrown to the ground and stepped on. She's disgusting and not good for anything." These words sank deep into Joan's heart, and the idea of premarital sex became detestable.

Then, as a sophomore in high school, Joan was raped. Her life fell apart. Not only did she suffer the trauma of being assaulted, but in her mind, she became like a piece of dirty, disgusting candy. She was afraid to tell her father, because she knew what he thought about girls who had sex. She concluded that she was worthless and had no future. She proceeded to have sex with any boy who happened along.

This behavior continued until Joan married in her late twenties. She still thought sex was disgusting and had no desire to make love with her husband. Since she thought sex was dirty, she did not see how it could be part of marriage, which was pure.

Annie, another woman, wrote me a note: "How do you deal with sex when you were raped as a child and see sex as a dirty and painful thing? I just can't seem to get it straightened out. I hate sex and will do anything not to have it."

It's easy to see how past sexual sins committed against you can affect your present life. Let's look at another example. Todd was only 12 years old when an older boy molested him. He often thought about this as he grew up and feared that this incident might mean he was a homosexual. Although Todd enjoyed making love with his wife, this thought continued to nag at him.

Perhaps you, too, have struggled with the repercussions of sexual abuse or rape. If you have, let me encourage you by saying that you can overcome the impact of these awful experiences. This chapter presents insights that have helped Joan, Annie, Todd and countless others overcome their past and move into a healthy sexual relationship with their spouse.

Although these pages will give you scriptural tools, *you are likely to need time to heal from past wounds*—time to pray, time to talk with a trusted friend and perhaps time to meet with a biblical counselor. For many, this chapter will only be a starting point on the path to healing.

Don't stay silent because of shame or embarrassment. Talk with someone. Seek a mature Christian of the same sex who will be willing to study these pages with you and to support you in prayer. Many before you have embarked on this journey of healing and have found themselves, in time, free from their ongoing pain.

Should Christians think about the past?

As you read the following pages, you may wonder if it is okay for you as a Christian to think about your past. You may fear that by doing so you are not trusting God. You may worry that you could get caught up in a never-ending cycle of analyzing what happened and why.

These are reasonable concerns. Some people spend far too much time examining past events. Others go so far as to manufacture false memories of abuse.

Yet if the past is still alive in your mind and affects how you function today, you need to deal with your thoughts and emotions. This chapter offers tools to help you move forward. With God's help, join Joan, Annie and Todd in finding freedom from the past.

 *Personal Application*

If you have been raped or sexually abused, describe the effects of these events on your attitudes about sex.

Now write a prayer asking God to help you gain insight and wisdom as you read the following pages—and to help you find freedom from the lingering effects of the abuse.

Healing from Sexual Abuse or Rape

Millions of people have been sexually abused or raped, often by someone they trusted. Most were women, but many men also have been victims. If you have been assaulted, be encouraged that even if your wounds go deep, God can heal you.

The following insights have helped many people in their healing process. After you read each point:

- Meditate on it.

- Answer the "Personal Application" questions.

- Ask God to make the insight real in your heart.

- Talk to a friend about it. Pray together.

Realize You Were a Victim

Do you feel responsible for the abuse or rape, thinking you deserved it or invited it? If so, you are not alone. It's common for a victim to say, "If I hadn't worn that dress, he wouldn't have touched me." Or, "If I hadn't gone out with him..." Or, "If I had just paid attention to the warning signs..."

Do not accept responsibility for the abuse.

Don't think it is your fault if you were raped or sexually abused. Even if you used poor judgment, do not excuse the abuser. Learn whatever lessons are necessary for the future, yet remember that no one has the right to rape or molest someone else—regardless of the circumstances.

Claire told me an all-too-common story of being sexually abused by her father when she was a young girl. When the abuse came out in the open, her father excused his behavior, saying she had invited it. When Claire saw me for counseling many years later, she still believed she was responsible for her father's actions.

It was hard for her to realize that her guilt was unreasonable, yet it was. When her father abused her, he was an adult and she was a child, physically unable to stop him. She was emotionally vulnerable. After all, he was her father, someone she trusted and obeyed. She was a victim.

If you were abused as a child, you may have asked yourself, "Why was I abused? Why not my sister? Was it something about me that caused him to choose me?" There are many possible answers to these questions. For example, you might have been more available at the time, you may have had a gentle personality or you may have reminded your abuser of someone else. Regardless of the answer, do not fall into the trap of thinking there is something bad about you, or that you deserved to be abused. You were a victim.

Do not condemn yourself if you did not resist.

Don't blame yourself if you did not resist. That does not mean you deserved to be raped or abused. You were a victim.

Do not condemn yourself if you kept it a secret.

Don't kick yourself if you didn't report the crime. You may have been afraid of the abuser, felt guilty, thought no one would believe you or felt it would be disloyal to the abuser if you told someone. Regardless of your reason for not reporting the crime, remember that you were a victim.

Remember that God hates abuse.

God's opinion about abusive treatment of any kind is clear. He points it out, condemns it and demands that we stand up for the victims.

Defend the cause of the weak and fatherless; maintain the rights of the poor and oppressed. Rescue the weak and needy; deliver them from the hand of the wicked (Psalm 82:3-4).

 *Personal Application*

If you have thought you invited or deserved rape or abuse, describe why you thought this.

Explain why these thoughts are not the truth.

Talk to God: *"Lord, I have believed a lie. Thank you for the truth. Please set me free from all feelings of shame, in Jesus' name."*

See the Abuser as Having Serious Problems

Abusers often are relatives, family friends, teachers, attorneys, counselors, pastors or others whom God expects to be supportive and loving. They misuse the victim's trust to do great evil. Many perpetrators use their superior physical strength or weapons to establish control. Others draw upon the force of their personalities.

If you were sexually abused or raped, you probably viewed the abuser as someone having greater power, either emotional or physical, than you. The result may be that you see yourself as inferior to this person.

The truth is that you aren't inferior to him or her. The abuser was a weak, flawed person who sinned. This person obviously came up short in integrity, wisdom and love. Ask God to help you stop looking at the perpetrator as a powerful, controlling person. Realize that he or she has serious personal problems.

 *Personal Application*

Have you thought of the abuser as superior to you?
❏ Yes   ❏ No

What is a more accurate way to view him or her?

_____

Do Not Minimize What Happened

Many minimize abuse, saying such things as, "He only touched me" or, "He didn't actually penetrate me." The common element in all such rationalizations is that the perpetrator could have done something worse.

However, even a "minor" incident can have a devastating impact and affect you throughout your life. The first step in healing may be to realize that what was done to you was significant, sinful and hurtful.

You may feel uncomfortable doing this because you do not want to judge someone else. Paul and John, writing about different types of sins, openly stated that they had been wronged by others (2 Timothy 4:14 and 3 John 9-10). This is not judging. It is appropriate to recognize sin as sin.

 *Personal Application*

Have you minimized the impact of past abuse?
❑ Yes   ❑ No

What statements have you made to minimize the abuse?

Why do you think you have minimized it?

What is the truth? Were you abused?

Do Not Feel Guilty if You Felt Some Pleasure

Many people were completely disgusted when they were abused. However, when I counsel victims, some say they experienced a degree of physical pleasure. They often say, "What's wrong with me? Why would I enjoy something as sick as that?"

If this describes you, don't feel guilty. There is nothing wrong with you. Your body simply responded to sexual stimulation.

Likewise, don't feel guilty if you experienced emotional pleasure. For example, if your father normally was distant, cold or angry, you might have felt a type of closeness when he sexually molested you. At the time, you may have desperately tried to see his actions as his way of expressing love. If you did, don't condemn yourself. It's understandable for a child to react that way in an effort to make sense out of a dreadful situation.

 *Personal Application*

Did you feel some emotional or physical pleasure when you were abused? ❑ Yes ❑ No

Explain why you should not feel guilty about this.

Realize You are Not "Damaged Goods"

Debbie was teary-eyed as she talked about being raped several months previously. She had been a virgin and now thought she was ruined. It did not take long to show her that in God's sight, she was still a virgin, and that the crime committed against her in no way made her impure.

Regardless of what was done to you, you are clean in God's eyes. Do not think of yourself as a second-class citizen. You are seated with Christ in heavenly places.

 And God raised us up with Christ and seated us with him in the heavenly realms in Christ Jesus (Ephesians 2:6).

 *Personal Application*

Have you felt like "damaged goods" because of sexual abuse or rape? ❏ Yes ❏ No

If so, write a prayer asking God to help you see yourself as cleansed and pure.

Do Not Think You are a Homosexual

If you were molested or raped by someone of the same sex, you may wonder why you were chosen. In fact, you may have lived for years tormented by lingering fears that you are a homosexual yourself.

Don't listen to those fears. The fact that someone chose to abuse you does not mean you are a homosexual. It simply means that you were abused.

 *Personal Application*

Have you worried that you are a homosexual because someone abused you? ☐ Yes ☐ No

Write a prayer renouncing that fear and asking God to give you peace in your heart.

Realize that Godly Sex is Very Different

When someone has been raped or sexually abused, he or she sometimes thinks that all types of sexual activity are bad or perverted. This attitude often carries over into marriage.

If this has been true for you, ask God to help you understand that when you were abused, the type of sex you experienced was radically different from the loving sexual union God intends for married couples. It was as different from pure sex as drowning in a tidal wave is different from swimming in the ocean.

 *Personal Application*

Ask God to help you deeply understand that sex within marriage is pure and holy, and that it is radically different from what you experienced when you were abused.

Take Appropriate Action

Jesus said, *"Love your enemies and pray for those who persecute you" (Matthew 5:44).* Does this mean you should not take action if you are raped? No. If you are raped, the most loving thing you can do is phone the police. This person needs to be stopped, for his or her own good as well as the good of others.

Calling the police is always the right thing to do if you have just been raped and is usually the best thing to do when you are sexually abused in other ways. However, there may be times when calling the authorities would not seem to be appropriate. Even in those situations, take some sort of action. For example, if you are a woman and your brother-in-law touches you inappropriately, confront him right away and tell your husband what happened.

Your actions will depend on the circumstances—for example, how long ago the abuse took place, what was done to you and the nature of your relationship with the abuser. Possible steps include alerting family members, confronting the abuser or contacting legal authorities. If you are unsure about what to do, talk with your pastor or a mature Christian friend.

The key is to be prepared to take action. Don't be silent simply because of embarrassment or fear that others will be upset because you say something.

Even if the abuse occurred a long time ago, it may be wise to talk to the perpetrator. For example, if your father molested you 40 years ago, and you have never talked about it with him, this secret may result in unspoken tension when you are together.

If you bring it up, he will have the opportunity to confess the sin and ask forgiveness. Your relationship could become much more honest. Then he could live with a clean conscience, knowing that you have forgiven him.

If he reacts in anger and you find yourself being treated by family members as a troublemaker, you have learned something valuable: Your family's "good feelings" were based on wishful thinking—not on reality. Pray that the Lord will turn their hearts around. In the meantime, get closer to your Christian family. Other members of the body of Christ are your true brothers and sisters.

✎ *Personal Application*

Should you talk with the abuser or report him or her to others? ❏ Yes ❏ No

List some steps you will pray about taking.

Forgive the Offender

Do not feel guilty if you were angry or depressed after you were abused. These are common reactions. However, regardless of what was done to you, deal with these emotions over time. If you are not careful, you can become an angry, bitter person. Bitterness is like cancer. It spreads and destroys. If it is not removed, it will make you spiteful, cynical and hard. You will not know the peace God intends for you.

The solution is both simple and difficult—learn to forgive and then move on with your life. Jesus gave us a remarkable example just before he died when he said, *"Father, forgive them, for they do not know what they are doing" (Luke 23:34).*

Study Ephesians 4:31-32 and Colossians 3:13, verses that encourage forgiveness. Ask God to help you forgive the perpetrator and stop dwelling on the injustice that was done to you.

When you forgive, you are not saying that what the perpetrator did was okay. You also are not saying that you will develop a friendship with him or her. And you are not saying you will not take appropriate action.

Forgive anyone who didn't believe your report.

If you reported sexual abuse or rape to your parents or others, and were met by disbelief, you may have felt angry or bitter. That reaction makes a lot of sense, yet you need to forgive those who didn't believe you, just as you need to forgive the perpetrator. When you do, you will experience God's peace in a new way.

 *Personal Application*

Are you willing to forgive your abuser? ❑ Yes ❑ No

If you are, write a brief statement to God expressing this decision, and then pray for help to forgive.

Look for Good to Come from Your Experience

The Bible says that *"in all things God works for the good of those who love him, who have been called according to his purpose" (Romans 8:28).* After time passes, good can result from your experience.

This, of course, is not to say that it was a good thing you had to go through the experience. Rather, it is to say that no matter what we go through, we can learn from our experiences.

The most common good that comes from rape or sexual abuse is understanding and compassion for others who are mistreated. Many who were abused later find themselves in a position to comfort other victims of abuse.

Praise be to the God and Father of our Lord Jesus Christ, the Father of compassion and the God of all comfort, who comforts us in all our troubles, so that we can comfort those in any trouble with the comfort we ourselves have received from God (2 Corinthians 1:3-4).

 *Personal Application*

What are possible ways that good may result from your abuse?

Is there some good you have already experienced? If so, what is it?

Healing from Immoral Advances

Although you may not have been physically assaulted, you may have been the victim of improper sexual advances. If so, these advances may have given you a negative view of sex.

Many teenage girls get the message that sex is the only thing that interests teenage boys. When on a date, they find themselves either fighting the boy off or giving in to his pressure. As girls grow into women, they discover the same pattern with many men—perhaps even with the man they eventually marry. As a result, women sometimes associate sex with this groping, predatory approach and think of it as disgusting.

When boys or men approach a woman that way, they are sinning. They are not displaying the respect and courtesy expected by God.

Men aren't the only ones who make immoral sexual advances, of course. Many women have been guilty of similar behavior.

Many of the insights about responding to rape and abuse in the previous pages can help someone deal with these memories. Forgiveness is a key. In addition, it can be helpful to realize that not all men (or women) behave that way—and that those who do can change.

Remember that this type of sexual pressure has nothing to do with the pure, loving sexuality God intends for married couples. God gives sexual drives. When directed by love and self-control within marriage, sexual desires are wonderful and holy. When not directed by true love, they can cause pain and revulsion.

If your feelings about sex have been damaged by predatory sexual practices, ask God to help you leave your old experiences behind and to move into a healthy, pure sexual relationship with your spouse.

This topic also applies to those who have been approached by homosexuals. If you have had this experience, or have been required to listen to ungodly teachings about sex in college or school, you may feel polluted. Seek God's help. He can cleanse your mind.

The impure advances that bother you may not have come from other people, but from your spouse. If your mate has approached you in objectionable ways, talk with him or her. Explain that you desire to have a wonderful sexual relationship, but this type of approach drives you away instead of attracting you. Invite your mate to study Chapter 5, "Set the Stage for Making Love," with you.

 *Personal Application*

If you need to deal with wounds from other people's predatory sexual practices, write a prayer asking God's help.

Healing from False Accusations

From time to time, a woman tells me how painful it was when her father wrongly accused her of being promiscuous. Or she tells me about the anger she felt when her mother accused her of dressing like a prostitute.

These and similar messages often have an extremely negative impact. In some cases, when a girl feels unfairly accused, she starts acting the way her parents seem to expect.

If your parents spoke to you like this, they might have thought you were acting in a way that would attract the wrong kind of attention, but didn't know how to talk about their concerns in a wise and loving way. Or perhaps they had confused feelings about their own sexuality, and didn't know how to respond to the sight of you growing up. Regardless of their reasons, forgive them and ask God to cleanse their messages from your mind.

Likewise, if one of your parents said you were acting like a homosexual, or someone said you were gay, forgive them and ask God to cleanse their messages from your mind.

 *Personal Application*

Did one or both of your parents wrongly accuse you?
❑ Yes ❑ No

If so, what was the accusation?

Write a prayer asking God to cleanse you from the impact of these words. Also tell him that you choose to forgive your father or mother.

Putting It All Together

Key point: Accept God's healing. He wants to give you peace.

•

Memory verse: *"He heals the brokenhearted and binds up their wounds" (Psalm 147:3).*

 *Action Plan*

Choose one or two things from this chapter to work on this week.

1.

2.

Chapter 4

Deal with
Your Sexual Sins

If we confess our sins, he is faithful and just and will
forgive us our sins and purify us from al
unrighteousness (1 John 1:9).

A re you having trouble with your sexual relationship? If so,
one reason could be your sexual sins, past or present. A
sobering principle, that of sowing and reaping, is found in Galatians 6:7-8. When a farmer sows seeds in a field, he or she
gets a crop. Likewise, when you sow "seeds" of behavior,
whether good or bad, you reap a crop of consequences.

John, a man I counseled, was frustrated about his sexual
relationship with his wife Sherry. Before they married, she
had been a passionate and adventuresome sexual partner.
Since they married, her interest and enthusiasm had faded to
almost nothing. He did not understand the drastic change.

Sexual sins have consequences.

John freely acknowledged that he and Sherry engaged in
sexual activities before marriage. He wasn't concerned about
that at all. He did not realize that sins have consequences.

 Do not be deceived: God cannot be mocked. A
man reaps what he sows. The one who sows to
please his sinful nature, from that nature will
reap destruction; the one who sows to please the

Spirit, from the Spirit will reap eternal life (Galatians 6:7-8).

Some results of sexual sins:

The following are some common consequences people experience because of sexual sins.

- If you and your spouse engaged in premarital sex, you may fear that he or she was only interested in sex and does not love you.

- If you and your spouse engaged in premarital sex, you may fear that your mate will have an affair, since he or she has already proved willing to have sex outside of marriage.

- If you and your spouse engaged in premarital sex, one or both of you may experience guilt or an ongoing sense of regret. This may result in thinking that sex is immoral, ugly or bad.

- If you had sexual activity with others before marrying, you may fantasize about them when you and your spouse make love.

- If you have watched pornography, read romance novels or books with sex scenes, watched TV or seen just about any movie, your thoughts about sex may have been polluted. These tainted thoughts can impact your attitudes about sex and lead to guilt, unholy fantasies or mistaken expectations. They may plague you for years, becoming intrusive and consuming.

- If you have had an abortion, or have encouraged someone else to have one, you may experience guilt or feel uncomfortable about sex.

- If you have engaged in same-sex activities or have fantasized about them, you may find yourself consumed by fears that you are a homosexual.

- If you have been sexually unfaithful since you married, you may feel guilty or distant from your spouse.

Read more about the consequences of sin in the fifth chapter of Proverbs, a chapter in which God warns against adultery and extols the joys of married sex. He concludes the chapter by saying that the evil deeds of a wicked man trap him and he *"will die for lack of discipline, led astray by his own great folly" (Proverbs 5:23).*

Personal Application

Have you engaged in sexual sins that affect your attitudes about sex?   ❑ Yes   ❑ No

In what ways have your sins affected your attitudes?

Ask God's Forgiveness

God desires to see us turn from sin and live pure lives. He will forgive you if you ask. Accept his forgiveness with thanks, and ask him for a pure, godly attitude about sexuality.

Wash away all my iniquity and cleanse me from my sin (Psalm 51:2).

If we confess our sins, he is faithful and just and will forgive us our sins and purify us from all unrighteousness (1 John 1:9).

Do not accept the devil's lies that you are a perverted person who can't change and who won't be forgiven by God. Whether your wrongdoing was adultery, homosexual behavior or any other type of sin, God desires to forgive, cleanse and transform you.

Personal Application

Do you need to ask God for his forgiveness and cleansing? ❑ Yes ❑ No

Are you ready to accept his forgiveness?
❑ Yes ❑ No

Talk to God: *"Lord, I confess my sins [name all your sexual sins] and ask for your complete forgiveness. I repent of these sins and ask you to make me clean. I am powerless to be free apart from the power of your Holy Spirit and I thank you for forgiving me. Thank you for making me whole and restoring the joy of my salvation. In Jesus' precious name, amen."*

Ask your Spouse's Forgiveness

If you have sinned against your spouse, ask his or her forgiveness. Also ask forgiveness if you have asked your mate to engage in sinful behavior such as watching pornography or participating in other immoral activities to "spice up" your sex life. Whatever the sin, your behavior has harmed your relationship.

Ask forgiveness for premarital sexual activity.

Steve and Mary looked at me with surprise. I had just suggested that each ask the other's forgiveness for their premarital sexual activities, something they had never thought of, since neither had forced the other to do anything. Yet by engaging in sexual activity, each had sinned against the other and needed to ask forgiveness. By doing this, they confronted their sin as sin and dealt with it in a biblical way.

If you engaged in premarital sexual activity with your spouse, ask forgiveness for it. Don't blame him or her for initiating the behavior or seducing you if you were a willing participant. Take responsibility for your behavior.

If your mate is willing, pray together and ask God to cleanse both of you from the effects of your sin.

 *Personal Application*

If you engaged in premarital sex with your spouse and have not asked forgiveness, write your plan to do so.

Ask forgiveness for sins since marriage.

An unconfessed sin is like an open wound. Until you take action to heal it, it festers and rots. Asking forgiveness is a key step to healing.

Confess secret sins.

If you have been engaging in a secret sin, your spouse may sense something is wrong, even if he or she is unaware of what you have been doing. You seem different—guilty, withdrawn or angry—and he or she doesn't understand what is going on. In most cases, the most honest and moral thing to do is to confess it and ask forgiveness.

 He who conceals his sins does not prosper, but whoever confesses and renounces them finds mercy (Proverbs 28:13).

Take the example of Henry and Jean, two people who came to me for counseling. Jean had not been aware that for years Henry had compulsively read pornography and masturbated several times a day. She had no idea why he showed little interest in making love. Self-doubt gnawed at her.

Over the years, her sense of failure became overwhelming as she tried to win his attention. Henry's sexual sin was compounded by not being honest with her. The result was a severely depressed wife and a disintegrating marriage.

Henry finally told his wife the truth and came in for counseling. With God's help, he overcame his sins, and they began the long process of building an honest relationship. It was extremely painful for them, yet their marriage became much stronger and both are glad the truth came out.

Does this principle mean you should confess every immoral thought or temptation? No. A general guideline is to ask forgiveness for (1) serious acts such as adultery or (2) any intrusive, repetitive conduct or thoughts that have a significant impact on your spouse or marriage.

If you have committed a serious sexual sin, such as having an affair, it may be a good idea to talk with a pastor or biblical counselor before talking with your spouse. It also may be wise to meet together with this person when you tell your spouse about your sin. Sexual betrayal can prompt extreme pain and anger. Your pastor or counselor can help you both talk and begin to rebuild your marriage.

You might fear confessing such sins, thinking your spouse will file for divorce. That is a possibility. However, as I consider the couples I have counseled, more marriages were saved when sins were confessed than when sins remained hidden. Most often, after the wounded spouse recovered from the initial pain, he or she was willing to forgive and rebuild the relationship. In any case, if your sins have seriously harmed your spouse, you owe it to him or her to explain what the real issues are.

 *Personal Application*

Do you need to ask your spouse's forgiveness for sexual sins? ❑ Yes ❑ No

Write your plan for talking with your spouse about your sins.

Win Back Your Spouse's Trust

Once you ask forgiveness, be prepared to be patient and understanding. If you have committed a serious sin, such as adultery, it probably will take time for your spouse to recover. Avoid saying, "You're a Christian so you must forgive me and forget about it." And don't simply say, "I won't do it again. Trust me." Instead, make an effort to understand why you sinned in the first place, learn how to walk in victory in the future and seek to win your spouse's trust.

Let your mate know that you are deeply repentant and willing to do whatever it takes to rebuild your marriage. If your spouse or pastor asks you to go to counseling or take other steps, do it. Demonstrate a teachable attitude. You need to learn new insights and patterns that will help you live victoriously.

If your mate left you because of your sin, do not pressure him or her to get back together. Instead, focus on the changes *you* need to make (Matthew 7:1-5). Ask God to help you become more Christ-like and give your spouse time to recover. *Win* his or her trust.

Personal Application

Are you prepared to patiently seek to *win* back your spouse's trust? ❑ Yes ❑ No

List three behaviors you will avoid.

1.

2.

3.

Now list godly patterns you will substitute for these behaviors.

1.

2.

3.

Overcome Sin

God told Cain, *"Sin is crouching at your door; it desires to have you, but you must master it" (Genesis 4:7).* Do not be lazy in your battle against sin. It may require an intense fight to master your temptations. However, although the compulsion to sin may feel overpowering, God provides a way out.

No temptation has seized you except what is common to man. And God is faithful; he will not let you be tempted beyond what you can bear. But when you are tempted, he will also provide a way out so that you can stand up under it (1 Corinthians 10:13).

Simply praying for freedom and waiting for a miracle is not enough. You must learn to practice self-control. Learning this is much like learning how to play soccer or any other physical sport. It takes practice. It requires time. It means making it a priority. You can learn to control your own body, but be prepared to work at it.

It is God's will that you should be sanctified: that you should avoid sexual immorality; that each of you should learn to control his own body in a way that is holy and honorable, not in passionate lust like the heathen, who do not know God (1 Thessalonians 4:3-5).

Control your thought life.

Sin begins in the mind (James 1:14), and it is in your mind that the battle must start. Identify and resist sinful thoughts or temptations the moment you experience them.

Temptation can be subtle and you can deceive you into thinking you aren't in danger. Do not tell yourself, "It's okay to fantasize a little, since I would never actually commit the sin." If you give yourself permission to enjoy sinful thoughts, you give those thoughts a foothold in your mind. Remember, sin is crouching at the door and it desires to have you.

Don't feel guilty because you have sinful thoughts—no one is ever completely free from temptation. What matters is that you resist the thoughts. They become sin only when you entertain them, rolling them around in your mind.

Your mind is a battlefield. The struggles are sometimes difficult, yet with the Lord's help, you can learn to focus on things that are pure and lovely. God will help you renew your mind.

 Offer your bodies as living sacrifices, holy and pleasing to God—this is your spiritual act of worship. Do not conform any longer to the pattern of this world, but be transformed by the renewing of your mind (Romans 12:1-2).

Make a "covenant with your eyes."

A good way to control your thought life is to monitor your eyes. Do not allow yourself to look at others in an impure way. Instead, follow the example of Job, who said, *"I made a covenant with my eyes not to look lustfully at a girl" (Job 31:1).*

Husbands, learn to look at other women as sisters in Christ or as people who need the Lord, not as sex objects. Wives, likewise, learn to look at other men as brothers in Christ or as people who need the Lord.

If you read or watch pornography, watch movies or read books with sexually explicit scenes, gaze at underwear ads, view immoral television sitcoms or look at anything else that glamorizes sexual immorality, stop! Exposing yourself to this is like drinking poison. It pollutes your thinking, giving you ungodly attitudes and false ideas about sex. It makes it extremely difficult to purely love your spouse.

If you can't control your viewing habits, disconnect the cable television service (or throw away your TV). Get off the Internet. Do whatever it takes.

I'm not just writing to men. Women, you too must monitor what you read and watch if you are to control your thought life. Throw away immoral "romance novels" and women's magazines with stories about illicit sex. Turn off the television when soap operas come on.

Do not rationalize sin.

Do you justify sin by saying it isn't really sin? Some say things such as, "We only had oral sex, not intercourse," or, "My spouse wouldn't make love, so it's not my fault I masturbated."

Others flirt with members of the opposite sex, then excuse themselves by saying they were joking or simply being friendly.

If you catch yourself rationalizing sin, treat it seriously. God calls us to dedicate ourselves to holiness.

 For God did not call us to be impure, but to live a holy life (1 Thessalonians 4:7).

Avoid dangerous situations.

Do not put yourself into any situation that might result in sin. Stay away from people who tempt or encourage you to do immoral things (1 Corinthians 5:11). Be wise when with people of the opposite sex. Avoid places that are dangerous for you. Be smart. Stay alert.

 So then, let us not be like others, who are asleep, but let us be alert and self-controlled (1 Thessalonians 5:6).

Flee temptation.

Paul gave simple yet effective instructions about how to respond to temptation: Flee. If you start to *really* like someone other than your spouse, pray for a new attitude and stay away from that person.

Flee the evil desires of youth, and pursue righteousness, faith, love and peace, along with those who call on the Lord out of a pure heart (2 Timothy 2:22).

Do not masturbate.

If you masturbate, you probably entertain sinful fantasies at the same time. Although masturbation is not explicitly forbidden in the Scriptures, the thoughts that usually accompany it are. Do not escape into a fantasy life. Determine that, with God's help, you will stop.

But I tell you that anyone who looks at a woman lustfully has already committed adultery with her in his heart (Matthew 5:28).

Sometimes people have orgasms in their sleep. If that happens to you, don't feel condemned. However, if you have sexually immoral dreams, ask God to give you pure dreams, instead.

Become accountable to others.

Members of the early church lovingly confronted one another when sin was manifested in their lives. Accountability to and support from leaders, as well as from other believers of the same sex, can be extremely helpful. Study James 5:14-16.

 *Personal Application*

Review these ways to resist sin and then write a plan to deal with any temptations you face.

Pursue Righteousness

Your battle against sin will not be successful if it simply is one of resisting sin. In addition to fighting *not* to do something, strive to *do* things that replace your sinful inclinations. Put off sin and put on righteousness.

As you devote more time to prayer, Bible study and fellowship, you will find that self-control becomes easier. This is because self-control is part of the fruit of the Spirit (Galatians 5:22-23). As you spend time with God, the fruit grows.

Draw close to God.

The most important preventive measure is to walk in God's Spirit. As Paul wrote, *"So I say, live by the Spirit, and you will not gratify the desires of the sinful nature" (Galatians 5:16).*

A key element of walking in the Spirit is to pray throughout the day. As Paul also wrote, *"Devote yourselves to prayer, being watchful and thankful" (Colossians 4:2).*

"Devote" is a strong word and lets us know how important prayer is. Pray not just to overcome sin, but also to know God better and to walk in his Spirit. Pray for others. Listen to God.

Another key is to read the Bible each morning and evening. It will cleanse and change you. You might want to join a Bible study group. Learning with others can help organize and motivate your Bible studies, much like joining a gym can help your exercise program.

> *How can a young man keep his way pure? By living according to your word. I seek you with all my heart; do not let me stray from your commands. I have hidden your word in my heart that I might not sin against you (Psalm 119:9-11).*

Love your spouse.

Take your eyes off your own desires and seek to express love in everything you do and say to your spouse.

Determine to stay faithful to your mate.

The Bible's standard is simple: Live a holy life, draw close to your spouse and refuse to engage in any sort of sexual activity unless it is with him or her.

> *Drink water from your own cistern, running water from your own well (Proverbs 5:15).*
>
> *Like a bird that strays from its nest is a man who strays from his home (Proverbs 27:8).*

Serve others.

Do not live a self-centered life, focusing on your own desires and struggles. Minister to others. You are God's workmanship and were created to do good works (Ephesians 2:10).

Train yourself to think about positive things.

I previously wrote about resisting impure thoughts. As you do so, replace them with pure thoughts.

Finally, brothers, whatever is true, whatever is noble, whatever is right, whatever is pure, whatever is lovely, whatever is admirable—if anything is excellent or praiseworthy—think about such things (Philippians 4:8).

Notice and appreciate the good things around you—the smell of dinner cooking, the graciousness of a friend, the loveliness of a sunset and a million other things.

Dress modestly when in public.

A woman reviewer of an early draft of this book wrote, "I think a note to women on proper attire might be good. Today's slinky 'hug' styles leave little to the imagination." She's right. Women (and men, too) who dress immodestly in public are violating God's Word. To get an idea about how seriously God looks at flirtatious behavior, read Isaiah 3:16-24.

Some women consciously dress to get men's attention. Take Sally, for example. When I counseled her and her husband Gregory, she told me that when she felt depressed, she put on a tight sweater and went to the mall so men would stare at her.

Margie, another woman who saw me for counseling, came to my office wearing an extremely form-fitting tee shirt. She complained that men frequently made sexual propositions and added that sometimes she gave in. When I suggested she dress more modestly, she reacted in anger: "I've worked out for one year to look like this, and I'm not going to hide it."

Both Sally and Margie knew what they were doing—they were looking for reactions from men.

If you go into the hallways of many churches, you can see lots of women who dress the same way. Some are like Sally and Margie, looking for attention. Others simply think they are being stylish and have no idea how their appearance affects men.

Does God want women to wear shapeless dresses that completely hide the fact that they are women? No, but he wants them to act and dress modestly.

 I also want women to dress modestly, with decency and propriety, not with braided hair or gold or pearls or expensive clothes (1 Timothy 2:9).

How short a skirt is permissible? How tight a blouse? To some degree, what's appropriate depends on the culture and situation (you probably wouldn't wear a swimsuit to church), so I can't give a rule that applies in every situation. But I can give some biblical principles:

- Put more attention on developing the inward beauty of a gentle and quiet spirit than on your outward appearance (1 Peter 3:3-4).

- Dress modestly when in public. It's fine to wear revealing clothes when with your husband in private, but your standards should be very different when in public.

- Do not imitate the world. Let someone else be on the forefront of immodesty.

> *Do not conform any longer to the pattern of this world, but be transformed by the renewing of your mind. Then you will be able to test and approve what God's will is—his good, pleasing and perfect will (Romans 12:2).*

- Don't do anything to cause others to stumble—in this case, men.

> *I try to please everybody in every way. For I am not seeking my own good but the good of many, so that they may be saved (1 Corinthians 10:33).*

Am I excusing some men's inappropriate sexual comments and behavior because of the way some women dress? No. They must answer to God for their actions. But women should look at their part and prayerfully consider how they dress.

Personal Application

Review the above points. What steps will you take to pursue righteousness?

Be Wise if Your Spouse Sins

The goal of this chapter is to encourage you to deal with your own sins. However, you may say, "I don't have any sexual sins, but my spouse does." If that's the case, the following guidelines will help you.

Do not join in your mate's sin.

Some people, when pressured by their spouse, are tempted to join in watching pornography or engaging in other sexual sins. Sometimes this is because they are lured by the sins. Other times they go along in an effort to win their mate's love. Sometimes they are afraid their spouse will leave them if they don't participate.

Regardless of your motive, do not sin. If you do, when you make love, you won't really be making love. You will only be having sex. You and your spouse will grow further apart emotionally, not closer. And you will be driving a wedge between yourself and God.

Follow Solomon's advice: *"My son, if sinners entice you, do not give in to them" (Proverbs 1:10).*

Don't take your spouse's sin personally.

Does your mate look at pornography or stare at others of the opposite sex? If so, this probably has very little to do with you. Most men have looked at women as sex objects at one time or another. Some women, likewise, have stared at men inappropriately. View this as a personal problem your mate needs to deal with, not as a rejection of you or your attractiveness.

Examine yourself.

Although you shouldn't take your mate's behavior personally, you should ask God if you contributed to the problem. It may be that you didn't, but it's possible you played a part. For example, if you refused to make love for a long time, then walked into a room and saw your spouse watching pornography, you should pray about your lack of availability.

 Do not deprive each other except by mutual consent and for a time, so that you may devote yourselves to prayer. Then come together again so that Satan will not tempt you because of your lack of self-control (1 Corinthians 7:5).

Along the same lines, if you ignored your mate emotionally or sexually for years and then discovered he or she had an affair, you should look at how you may have helped set up the situation.

Your spouse's sins might not have anything to do with you, of course. Sin has a power of its own, and your mate may have given in to it regardless of how good a spouse you were. I've observed that to be the case with many men caught up in pornography, men who had no complaint about their wives yet who gave in to sin.

In any case, even if you came up short in some areas, *your actions do not excuse your spouse's sins.* Your mate must answer to God for his or her sins, regardless of what you did.

Lovingly confront the sin.

By encouraging you not to take your spouse's sins personally, I'm not suggesting you do nothing. If your mate stares at other people, looks at pornography or engages in other sexual sins, it is appropriate to lovingly confront this behavior.

Be supportive if your mate confesses a sin.

Several years ago, Skeeter and I invited a friend and his wife to dinner. When Skeeter and the wife were in another room, my friend told me that he had woken his wife up at 1:30 that morning to tell her he'd been getting up at night for several months to watch pornography and masturbate. He said he was deeply ashamed, asked her forgiveness and said he wanted to overcome the sin. Her immediate response was to forgive him and join him in prayer.

Although it's not always easy to respond as quickly as she did, her actions provide a good example. If sin comes out in the open, you are likely to react with anger and a sense of betrayal.

That's normal. Yet good can come out of the situation. When someone confesses a sin, a step is taken toward healing. When a sin is hidden, it is silently destroying the marriage. The two of you now have the opportunity to deal honestly with what's going on—to pray and grow together, making your marriage stronger than ever before.

 All things work together for good to them that love God, to them who are the called according to his purpose (Romans 8:28).

What if your spouse has an affair? Although you have scriptural grounds to divorce (Matthew 19:9), it's usually better to rebuild the marriage. However, if your mate is unrepentant and continues to have affairs, you may need to meet with your pastor and take stronger steps.

 *Personal Application*

If your mate has sinned sexually, which of the above points will help you?

Putting It All Together

Key point: Confess and turn from your sins, both in thought and action.

•

Memory verse: *"If we confess our sins, he is faithful and just and will forgive us our sins and purify us from all unrighteousness" (1 John 1:9).*

 *Action Plan*

Choose one or two things from this chapter to work on this week.

1.

2.

Chapter 5

Set the Stage
for Making Love

Come away, my lover (Song of Songs 8:14).

Before pitching in a baseball game, the pitcher must warm up. Before making a presentation to a client, the salesperson needs to obtain an interview. Prior to throwing a dinner party, the host and hostess clean the house, prepare food and perhaps select music.

If the pitcher doesn't warm up, he or she may pull a muscle. If the salesperson doesn't work to get an interview, there may be no chance to make the sales pitch. If the host and hostess leave the house a mess and let the guests go hungry, the guests may leave the party early.

Making love has one thing in common with each of these activities. It requires sensitive attention to setting the stage. If you prepare carefully and lovingly, you are much more likely to have a wonderful time. If you prepare sloppily or not at all, there may not be a party.

Be Tender throughout the Day

As I wrote in Chapter 2, sex is most enjoyable when it is the result and expression of an ongoing, loving relationship. If you criticize or ignore your spouse during the day, then expect romance at night, you are likely to be disappointed. If you build a foundation of friendship, respect and romance, you will experience a much more intimate and satisfying sexual relationship. If you haven't already done so, read Chapter 2 before studying this one.

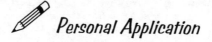 *Personal Application*

Write three actions that your spouse finds loving and romantic.

1.

2.

3.

Be sensitive when you hug or talk about sex.

Your mate may resent it if you touch him or her sexually throughout the day. On the other hand, he or she may enjoy sexual touches. Discover what your spouse likes and dislikes, then show your love by respecting these wishes.

Likewise, be sensitive when talking about sex. If your mate enjoys hearing sexual comments throughout the day, feel free to express them. If not, talk about something else.

 *Personal Application*

What words or actions make your spouse feel loved?

What words or actions push your spouse away?

Praise your spouse.

Most people have felt insecure about their appearance and desirability at one time or another. Be sensitive to this, and look for things to praise in your mate. Don't criticize sensitive aspects of your spouse's appearance, such as the size of your wife's breasts or your husband's penis. Such words leave cruel wounds that are hard to heal.

Focus instead on praise, as in the Song of Songs, where the wife said, *"How handsome you are, my lover! Oh, how charming" (Song of Songs 1:16).* Her husband complimented her by saying, *"How beautiful you are, my darling! Oh, how beautiful" (Song of Songs 4:1).*

Your spouse might look like a skinny chicken or have crooked teeth. Not many of us look like movie stars. Ask God to help you focus on the good things and praise them. Let him give you eyes to see in each other the beauty you have in his sight.

 *Personal Application*

What are some things for which you will praise your spouse?

Get Enough Rest

Fatigue and stress are twin enemies of sexual intimacy. Suggestions to help you deal with stress are sprinkled throughout this book. They include going on dates, praying together and talking before you make love.

In addition to taking these steps, be sure to get enough sleep. Although some people sleep too much, many of us (including me) tend to take on more than we should and deprive ourselves of the rest God wants us to enjoy.

 In vain you rise early and stay up late, toiling for food to eat—for he grants sleep to those he loves (Psalm 127:2).

 *Personal Application*

Do you need to sleep more? ❑ Yes ❑ No
Does your mate need to sleep more? ❑ Yes ❑ No

If you answered "yes" to either question, talk with your spouse. What will you do to be sure each of you gets enough sleep?

Approach Your Mate Romantically

Eric often announced he wanted to make love by saying, "Let's get nasty." When his wife Barbara gave him the cold shoulder, he felt sorry for himself and thought she was passionless.

James, another frustrated husband, grabbed his wife's breasts and made gross sexual comments throughout the day to let her know he was in the mood. She always reacted with disgust, so he moved into a separate bedroom, certain that she didn't love him.

Neither man understood the importance of approaching his spouse gently and respectfully. Each woman felt as if she were a sex object, not a beloved wife.

The way you approach your spouse—your actions and your words—make a big difference. Let's look at some wiser, more sensitive ways to initiate a romantic time together.

Speak sensitively when you bring up sex.

Imagine that you have been sweet and tender to your spouse for several days and would like to make love. What is the best way to bring it up? If you speak gently, using words of love and tenderness, you set the mood for an enjoyable, romantic time. If you are pushy or use insensitive language, you are likely to repel your mate. The way you approach your spouse has a big impact on his or her response.

A bad way to start is to quote 1 Corinthians 7:3-5 and demand sex. If you say, "I have a right to your body," your mate will feel like running away.

"But," you might object, "Don't those verses say neither spouse should deprive the other of sexual intimacy?" Yes, the Bible says that. However, this command, which is discussed later in this chapter, is perverted if you say, "I own your body and you must do what I want." When you speak like this, your mate feels like an object, not someone who is loved.

As you and your spouse grow together, you may develop your own unique ways to initiate sex. In the case of one couple I know, the amorous person says, "Let's order out for pizza tonight." This is not only a code. They actually order a pizza so they can eat early, dispense with cleaning dishes and get to bed at a decent time.

Identify how your mate would like to be approached.

If you do not know how your spouse would like to be approached in words or touch, ask for guidelines. People are different, and your husband or wife may respond to a different type of approach than you would. You might prefer to hear, "Let's order pizza," while your mate would prefer you to unbutton his or her shirt as you say loving words of invitation.

There are no absolute rules about how to initiate sex, but there is an absolute law, and that is the law of love. If you truly desire to express love to your spouse:

- Do not say or do anything to present sex in an impure light. For example, avoid saying, "Let's get nasty."

- Learn what makes your spouse feel loved and then approach him or her in that manner.

 *Personal Application*

How do you approach your spouse when you want to make love?

Ask your mate how he or she would like you to initiate sex. Write the answer here.

_____

Create a pleasing environment.

Is it important to your spouse to make love in a clean bedroom? Is background music, candlelight, silk sheets or something else special to him or her?

Perhaps your mate has trouble enjoying making love when the kitchen is a mess. If so, help clean it.

Get to know what matters. The more sensitive you are to your spouse's desires, the more pleasurable your sexual intimacy will be.

 *Personal Application*

What type of physical environment increases your mate's enjoyment of sex?

Pay attention to your appearance.

Joe complained that his wife didn't want to make love. Irene explained this was because he was dirty and smelly after working hard all day. She said she would be glad to make love if he would take a bath or shower. Joe refused, saying he was insulted because she did not "love him as he is."

In another couple, the roles were reversed. After a hard day's work, Jessica refused to take a bath before making love, although her husband Lance tried to diplomatically point out it would increase his pleasure. She was upset because she wanted to be "natural."

Nonsense! Washing, shaving (unless you have a beard) and brushing your teeth make it much more pleasant for your mate. Your main task is to please your spouse. Pay attention to your personal appearance. Stay in good physical condition, exercising and eating healthy food.

Wives, enjoy your husband's enjoyment.

Men are visually stimulated. There's no need to be insulted by your husband's appreciative gaze. Solomon, in the Song of Songs, went on and on about the beauty of his bride. She had good things to say about his looks, too.

God created your husband with a desire to enjoy your beauty. Wear a negligee that he likes. Wear perfume if he enjoys it. (Solomon and his bride were big fans of perfume.) Don't be embarrassed and hide your nakedness from him. You are a painting that God has given him to enjoy. Take pleasure from his enjoyment of you.

Don't hide the painting, thinking you are not beautiful. Don't be embarrassed if you have had a mastectomy or think of any other part of yourself as "flawed."

What if you are overweight?

It's hard not to react if your spouse says he or she wishes you would lose weight. I know it bothered me one night when

Skeeter teased me by saying my potbelly reminded her of a pregnant guppy.

Most of us probably feel insulted if our mate complains about our weight, even if we know our spouse is right. We want to be loved for ourselves, not for our outer appearance.

We may be irritated because society puts *way* too much emphasis on weight, especially for women. Not only that, we may be frustrated because we wish we were thinner, but have had trouble losing weight and keeping it off. Our mate's words can sound cruel and unloving.

It's common for people, when their spouse complains about their weight, to get mad and refuse to try to lose weight. In fact, they often start eating more, seemingly to spite their mate.

While such anger is understandable, it's not the way God wants us to respond. If your spouse complains about your weight, don't react with angry speeches and eating binges. Instead, if you want to say something, have a gentle, serious talk, saying how the words hurt. Explain that speeches about weight loss do not help you get thinner.

Then go to the Lord. Ask him if you should change your eating or exercise habits. If he says "yes," make plans and ask for his help to make needed changes.

Seek to look attractive to your spouse, but don't be consumed by guilt or self-loathing if you are overweight. The quality of your walk with God is much more important than how you look (1 Timothy 4:7-8). Avoid worshipping at the altar of physical beauty. Take comfort in the fact that God loves you.

The words of King Lemuel, although written about a woman, also apply to men:

 Charm is deceptive, and beauty is fleeting; but a woman who fears the LORD is to be praised (Proverbs 31:30).

Avoid comparing yourself to others. There always will be people who, according to our culture's standards, are more handsome or beautiful than you. Reject these standards and think about the fact that God made you, and you are beautiful in his sight.

Don't be embarrassed about growing older. As you age, wrinkles appear, various parts of your body sag and your muscles lose tone. Instead of being distressed by these changes, accept them as natural. Enjoy growing in the Lord and approaching the time when you will be with him forever.

Stay balanced.

Try to look attractive for your mate, yet don't think you must do everything he or she wants. For example, Melissa told me that she had her breasts enlarged for her husband, but he wasn't satisfied with their size. He demanded she have another operation to make them "as big as melons." He threatened divorce if she refused.

When she asked me if she should do what he wanted to show she loved him, I responded, "No." My reasoning: (1) His demands were extremely unreasonable and unloving, (2) he had personal problems and didn't understand how to love and (3) he would probably continue to make other similar demands if she gave in. I showed her that the Bible tells us to love *"in knowledge and depth of insight" (Philippians 1:9).* Sometimes the wisest and most loving thing to do is to gently say, "No."

✏️ *Personal Application*

What steps will you take to appear pleasing to your spouse?

_____

Do not criticize your spouse's weight.

Let me add a word of caution to the husband or wife of an overweight person: If you wish your spouse would lose weight, don't withhold your love or try to force your mate to go on a diet. *God loves your spouse as is and wants you to love him or her that way too.*

When I was a young husband, after Skeeter had our second child, she failed to regain her earlier shape and I got upset. One time, I got angry because she was eating ice cream, so I flushed the remains of a half-gallon of ice cream down the toilet.

She was understandably hurt. I defended my actions, but over time I realized how immature and unloving I had been. I prayed, and God gave me the eyes to see her beauty just as she was. I asked her to forgive me, and she did.

Do you have complaints about your spouse's appearance? If so, or if you are not sexually attracted to your mate, pray for God's help to love your spouse just as he or she is. Break free of the tyranny of outward appearances and learn how to truly love, regardless of your mate's physical condition.

If you are worried about your spouse's health, first make sure he or she feels secure in your love. Once you have given the clear message that you love him or her, on rare occasions it may be a good idea to tactfully voice your concern.

Pray for an understanding and compassionate attitude before talking. It is hard for most people to lose weight and keep it off. After you speak, don't nag. Leave your mate in God's hands.

 *Personal Application*

Write a short prayer, asking God to help you love your spouse just as he or she is.

Take Turns Initiating Sex

Who usually initiates making love in your marriage? In most marriages, the husband usually is the initiator, but in some families, the wife takes the first step.

If your spouse usually makes the first move, he or she probably would enjoy it if you sometimes got things started. Take the initiative now and then. Once you get used to it, you will find that this role reversal makes lovemaking more exciting for both of you.

Wives, feel free to take the first step.

Some think that only the man should initiate sexual activities. That's not what the Bible says. Read the first four verses of the Song of Songs, a passage that beautifully illustrates a wife's passionate desire for her husband.

In verse two, she takes the initiative by asking him to kiss her: *"Let him kiss me with the kisses of his mouth—for your love is more delightful than wine"* (Song of Songs 1:2). In verse 4, she asks him to take her away and adds that she's in a rush when she says, *"Let us hurry"* (Song of Songs 1:4).

 *Personal Application*

What percentage of the time do you initiate making love? (0% - 100%) _____

What percentage of the time does your mate initiate it? (0% - 100%) _____

Talk with your spouse. Are you both comfortable with this? Would either one like to see a change? Write your plans here.

_____

Be Wise in Your Timing

Timing is important when you make love. A common example of someone with bad timing is the husband who watches TV all night while his wife cooks dinner, takes care of the kids and cleans the house. Then, at the end of the evening, when she is exhausted, he expects her to become his passionate lover. She would be much more receptive if he helped with the housework and children during the evening and made plans to go to bed earlier.

Another example of bad timing is the wife who wants to make love when her husband comes in exhausted after working hard all day. Instead of feeling insulted if he doesn't seem interested, she could ask if he would like to take a nap or soak in the bathtub.

A third example of bad timing is the husband who wakes his wife in the middle of the night with sexual caresses. Although some women enjoy this, the vast majority of women who have discussed this in my counseling office say it makes them feel violated or used, not loved.

When should you make love? There is no "correct" time of day. Some enjoy mornings, while others enjoy evenings. Some find it romantic to go out for dinner before making love. Others dislike sex on a full stomach and prefer making love before going out. Talk with each other about your desires. Try to find times that are comfortable for both. If your wishes are very different, be willing to compromise, sometimes making love when he wants, sometime when she wants.

Be sensitive to your spouse's desires and your circumstances. For example, if one of you plans to leave on a business trip tomorrow, make love tonight. This is a wonderful way to reaffirm your love and to send the traveler off with both of you free from sexual tension.

There are times, of course, when you should be willing to go without making love. Some examples might be during the wife's menstrual period or when one of you is exhausted, suffering pain, sick or depressed.

 *Personal Application*

Are you sensitive about *when* you initiate sexual relations? ❑ Yes ❑ No

Ask your spouse when he or she would like to make love. Write his or her answer here.

Be Available

God's basic principle is that your body belongs to your spouse as well as to yourself. Each should be available to the other. Notice the woman's open invitation to her husband in the Song of Songs:

Let my lover come into his garden and taste its choice fruits (Song of Songs 4:16).

You are responsible to do everything you can to fulfill your mate sexually. This involves prioritizing your sexual relationship. It means letting your husband or wife know you are available to make love. And it often means planning ahead.

The husband should fulfill his marital duty to his wife, and likewise the wife to her husband. The wife's body does not belong to her alone but also to her husband. In the same way, the husband's body does not belong to him alone but also to his wife. Do not deprive each other except by mutual consent and for a time, so that you may devote yourselves to prayer. Then come together again so that Satan will not tempt you because of your lack of self-control (1 Corinthians 7:3-5).

The truth of these verses can be seen in most people's daily lives. If you and your spouse go a long time without making love, it probably puts a strain on one or both of you.

Husbands often feel hurt, rejected and unloved when their wife says "no" to making love. The same can be true for women.

When I met with Carolyn and Gary, she mentioned several ways in which she tried to get Gary's interest, ranging from greeting him at the door wearing a negligee to lighting candles in their bedroom. He responded to her efforts by laughing. She felt humiliated and rejected.

If you frequently rebuff your spouse's sexual advances—whether you are the husband or the wife—you may be unaware of how much misery you are inflicting. Rejection is one of the toughest things for most of us to handle. When you say "no," it often sounds like, "I don't love you." Many people go through life feeling deeply unloved, hurt, angry or frustrated because their spouse seems disinterested in sex.

The Bible stresses mutual availability, yet that doesn't mean you must always respond instantaneously to your spouse's overtures. If you are about to serve your family dinner and your mate says, "Let's make love," reply, "I'd love to, but let's wait until dinner's over and the kids are in bed."

 *Personal Application*

How available are you when your spouse desires to make love? Score yourself from 0 to 10.

0   1   2   3   4   5   6   7   8   9   10
Not very available   Very available

If you have not been very available, write a prayer asking God's forgiveness. Also ask him to help you respond enthusiastically.

Wives, do not be put off by his sex drive.

Do you sometimes feel hurt, thinking your husband only loves you for your body? Have you ever complained, "All you think about is sex?" If so, you are not alone. Many women voice similar complaints.

Biological drives are real. Do not blame your husband for them. After all, they are God-given. Steer clear of thinking your husband is an animal or that there is something wrong with him if he feels an urge to make love more often than you do.

Imagine that he had not eaten for one week. Now imagine that he came home and saw a delicious meal that was forbidden to him. As he went through the evening, how could he avoid thinking about eating? You would be cruel if you held a bowl of soup in his face and said, "All you think about is food. Let's get off that subject and talk about something else." If you haven't made love for a while and your husband begins to focus on sex, be understanding. Make love that night.

Even if you made love last night, be gracious if your husband pays you a sexual compliment today. It's his way of saying, "I love you."

However, if sex is all he talks about, it is okay to gently point that out and request some additional conversational topics. Likewise, if his comments are crude or offensive, explain how they affect you and ask him to use different words.

You may be thinking, "My husband isn't starving. We make love a lot, but he wants to make love *all* the time." If that is the case, it may be appropriate to set some limits or seek outside help.

Bill and his wife Margaret got together with me because he was frustrated about their sex life. He got right to the point and asked me to tell her that men have biological needs. Margaret responded, "We make love six times a day. I think that should be enough."

The problem was not Margaret's "unavailability." It was Bill's compulsive desires. As you will read later, there are times when it's okay to say, "No."

Husbands, be available to your wife.

The Bible instructs husbands, as well as wives, to be available (1 Corinthians 7:3-5). Although it's more common for a man to complain about his wife not being available, it is not unusual for a woman to voice frustration. Some men frequently say they don't want to make love. Others insist upon making love on their timetable.

 *Personal Application*

Have you resented your spouse's sex drive?
❑ Yes ❑ No

If you answered "yes," write a prayer asking God to forgive you and to help you be more sensitive to your mate's desires.

Discuss each other's desired frequency.

Desire for sex varies depending on stress, personality and circumstances.

If you are nursing a child, your energy may be drained and your sexual interest may be less than it once was. Not co-incidentally, your husband's desire and frustration level may be higher than ever.

Your age also may affect your desire for sexual intimacy. Many couples discover that the husband is more interested in the early years of marriage, while the wife is more interested in the later years. Then, when women go through menopause, they sometimes find their sexual desire lessens, unless they are taking estrogen or herbal equivalents.

Discuss each other's feelings and be prepared to compromise. Each should look not only to his or her own interests, but also to the spouse's interests (Philippians 2:4).

Be honest with yourself when you talk. If you make love frequently, yet still are consumed by sexual urges, you may be using sex for the wrong reasons. For example, you may be seeking reassurance of your spouse's love or trying to feel better because of problems at work.

On the other hand, if you have little interest in sex, look at the reasons why. You may need to get more sleep or cut back on some of your commitments.

 *Personal Application*

How frequently would you like to make love?

What are your spouse's desires?

Talk together to make a plan that each is comfortable with. Write it here.

Do not subtly deprive your spouse.

Avoid putting up a wall that says, "Stay away from me. I'm not interested in sex." For example, as bedtime approaches, do not withdraw emotionally or start a fight. Once in bed, don't pretend you don't understand what your spouse is doing if he or she starts to caress you in a way that means, "I'd like to make love." Either be available or have a straightforward discussion (as described later in this chapter).

Personal Application

Do you subtly deprive your spouse? ☐ Yes ☐ No

Describe how you do this and what you will do differently in the future.

Respond lovingly when you are approached.

Say "yes" when your spouse suggests making love, even if sex is not the number one thing on your mind. If you like to plan ahead for intimacy and your mate wants to be more spontaneous, pray for grace to be responsive. Although dealing with a different subject, Paul stated a basic Christian principle when he wrote, *"God loves a cheerful giver"* (2 Corinthians 9:7).

✎ *Personal Application*

Do you need to respond to your spouse's advances more enthusiastically? ❑ Yes ❑ No

How will you respond the next time your spouse shows a desire to make love?

"But I don't feel close to my spouse."

A woman handed me a note during the break of a marriage class I was teaching. It said, "If a wife knows her husband does not value her as a person and, because of his pathological illness, he cannot cherish her, does the wife have the option of not engaging in sex with her husband? How can she handle this situation without prostituting herself?"

Many women (and a few men) have asked similar questions in my counseling office. It's easy to see why. Most of us enjoy making love a lot more when we feel emotionally close to our spouse. As I wrote in Chapter 2, a close friendship provides a solid foundation for sexual intimacy.

However, what do you do when you don't feel emotionally close to your mate? Perhaps your spouse has been distant or angry. Maybe he or she has approached you crudely. If so, you might feel the deep sense of alienation described by the woman who gave me the note.

If you are like many people, when you don't feel close to your spouse, you may think it's wrong, immoral or unspiritual to be sexually intimate.

That's not the way God looks at it. You can see this if you study God's principles of loving without keeping a record of wrongs (1 Corinthians 13:5), forgiving (Colossians 3:13), returning a blessing for a curse (1 Peter 3:9), being sexually available (1 Corinthians 7:3-5) and doing everything wholeheartedly as unto the Lord (Ephesians 6:7).

Don't use sex as a weapon or hold back from being sexually intimate, saying, "I'll be nice to you when you are nice to me." Instead, approach lovemaking as a way to reach out, to increase your sense of closeness and to build a bridge between the two of you. Put your whole heart into it. Minister love to your spouse. If you make love with a loving attitude, you will find yourself drawing closer to your mate emotionally—even if he or she remains distant. Christ demonstrated his love to us when we were unlovely. Do the same for your mate.

I'm not suggesting you shouldn't talk with your spouse about your feelings. If you feel a distance between yourself and your mate, it may be appropriate to say, "Yes, let's make love, but I'd like to talk about something first." However, seek God's help to love your mate, regardless of how he or she responds.

✐ *Personal Application*

Do you think making love with your spouse when you are emotionally distant can sometimes build a bridge between you? ❑ Yes ❑ No

Why did you answer the way you did?

Gently say "no" when appropriate.

It's not always possible or necessary to make love at a moment's notice. If you are about to go to work, and your spouse says, "Let's make love," gently respond, "I can't right now, but let's do it later." If you are sick or exhausted, say so. However, also say you will be available in the future.

If you strongly do not want to make love—for example, if you feel like screaming when your spouse touches you—it may be appropriate to say no to your mate's request and then seek outside help. You could say, "I feel like screaming when you touch me and just can't make love with you. But I don't want to leave it there. I know we have serious problems and

I'm willing to work on them. Let's talk with our pastor or a biblical counselor."

This kind of response also would be appropriate if you are married to someone like Bill, the man who wanted to make love more than six times a day. His desires had little to do with love and much to do with personal problems. In such a case, it is wise to set limits and to suggest counseling.

If your spouse becomes pushy and says, "Your body belongs to me," you could respond by saying, "Yes, but your body belongs to me, and I want it to run away from me as fast as it can!"

 *Personal Application*

When you say "no," do you do so lovingly?
❑ Yes ❑ No

What do you say?

What changes do you need to make in how, and how often, you say, "No"?

Respond wisely if your spouse says, "No."

You may react with self-pity or anger if your spouse rebuffs your sexual advances. Yet these are exactly the reactions that God wants you to avoid. The Bible says, *"Love is patient, love is kind ... it is not easily angered, it keeps no record of wrongs" (1 Corinthians 13:4-5).* If you react with anger or self-pity, it reveals a lack in *your* love. Instead of being upset, respond with wisdom and love.

Although he was writing about a different kind of trial, James gave us a powerful principle when he wrote:

Consider it pure joy, my brothers, whenever you face trials of many kinds, because you know that the testing of your faith develops perseverance. Perseverance must finish its work so that you may be mature and complete, not lacking anything (James 1:2-4).

When you are rebuffed, you have an opportunity to develop a deeper love and grow in self-control. Pray, "Thank you God for the opportunity to grow in love and patience. Please help me become more loving and self-controlled."

Evaluate yourself.

Although you may not have done anything wrong, your behavior may be partly responsible for your spouse's lack of interest. Ask yourself the following questions to see if you are partly responsible:

❑ Have you ignored your mate?

❑ Have you been critical?

❑ Have you been romantic?

❑ Have you talked about things that matter?

❑ Do you have unresolved problems that need to be discussed?

❑ Did you watch TV while your spouse cooked dinner, cleaned the kitchen and helped the children with their homework?

❑ Did you wait until it was late at night to make love?

Husbands, if your wife rebuffs you, she may be upset because you've been criticizing or ignoring her. Work on your friendship. Get involved in her life in a positive way throughout the day.

Wives, if your husband rebuffs you, he may struggle with a poor self-concept, be insecure in your love or think he is not a good lover. Encourage and honor him throughout the day. Remember that *"the wife must respect her husband"* (*Ephesians 5:33*).

 *Personal Application*

Do you react with anger or self-pity when your spouse says, "No"? ❑ Yes ❑ No

How will you respond in the future?

Make Plans to Make Love

Many couples have so many demands on their time, or such busy schedules, that there never seems to be a convenient time to make love. When one voices an interest, the other is likely to respond, "I'm too busy" or "I'm too tired."

If this describes you, plan ahead. Make a date for romance. There is nothing wrong or unromantic about this. In fact, if both are so busy that neither desires to make love, schedule time for it anyway. Your lives are out of balance and you need to reconnect.

Take the case of Ted and Debby. Ted complained to Debby that he wasn't a high enough priority in her life. When she asked him to be more specific, he said he wanted to make love more often. At the time, they had one child. Debby worked a full-time job. She also did all the housework and took care of their child after work hours. She was exhausted much of the time and seldom in the mood to make love.

But when she prayed about it, she knew Ted was right. She hadn't made him a priority, so she came up with a proposed plan: Ted would be in charge of their love life. They would make love whenever he wanted, as long as he scheduled their "dates" in advance.

Debby figured that with advance warning, she could save energy for lovemaking. And—this was her stroke of genius—she requested that on lovemaking nights, Ted would take care of the baby for three hours during the early evening so she could nap, read or whatever. He quickly agreed. The result: They've never made love so often and she's more rested than she has been in years.

Even if you do not have a busy schedule, you might benefit from planning ahead if one of you has trouble making love on a moment's notice. Although some people enjoy making love spontaneously, others do not. They feel more comfortable preparing emotionally throughout the day. Or they have a ritual they like to follow such as going for a walk or talking before becoming sexually intimate. If this is true for you or your spouse, discuss your desires earlier in the day.

If you have not planned ahead before, you may feel awkward the first few times you make love at a scheduled time. Don't worry. You will learn to enjoy it. In fact, you may come to especially appreciate these times.

Personal Application

If you and your spouse have trouble finding time to make love, get together and write a plan.

Follow through on your plans.

Nancy laughed as she told me how she had teased her husband the previous night. Earlier in the day, she had told him she would make love that evening. Then as night fell, she bantered with him, saying, "Maybe I will, but maybe I won't." Her eyes twinkled as she recounted what she thought was a good joke. But then she sobered up as she said how hurt he had seemed. She had no idea why he reacted that way.

Lucy was equally insensitive to her husband. They would often talk during the day and agree to make love in the evening. More often than not, however, she forgot the conversation and acted surprised when he voiced his desire at night.

Neither of these women realized how cruel they had been. One made a joke out of something that was very important to her husband. The other showed indifference. Both left their husband dealing with the pain of rejection.

 *Personal Application*

Do you sometimes make a commitment to make love and then not treat it seriously?   ❑ Yes   ❑ No

How will you remind yourself to be more considerate in the future?

Be open to spontaneous lovemaking, too.

Although planning ahead can enhance your sexual enjoyment, there's no reason to plan ahead every time. Making love spontaneously can be thrilling. If you feel awkward about making love spontaneously, pray to be more flexible and to learn to enjoy these times.

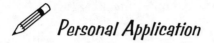 *Personal Application*

If you have trouble making love spontaneously, write a prayer asking God to help you be more flexible.

Now make a plan to surprise your spouse by initiating making love unexpectedly one time this week.

Pray Before Making Love

Do you pray before eating dinner? Probably. Do you pray for God's blessing before making love? Probably not. Yet making love is no less significant than eating breakfast, lunch or dinner. Pray silently, as an individual, or pray together if your spouse would like to join you. Pray that God will:

✓ Bless your time of making love.

✓ Help you *love* your spouse.

✓ Help you enjoy your spouse's love.

✓ Free you from worries and life's stresses.

✓ Give you pure thoughts.

✓ Deliver you from resentment toward your mate.

✓ Help you focus on giving your mate pleasure.

✓ Help you be passionate and free of inhibitions.

 *Personal Application*

Write your plans to pray, individually or as a couple, before you make love.

Talk Before Making Love

Sometimes it's fun to make love spontaneously and quickly. However, if you usually talk for a while before being sexually intimate, you will find yourselves connecting emotionally and feeling closer as you make love.

This can be true when your marriage has been going well, but it's especially true when there has been tension in your marriage. It's also true if either of you has been experiencing job stress, frustration with the kids or disappointment over any number of things. Unless you talk first, either or both of you may be too distracted to enjoy sexual intimacy.

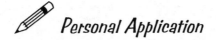 *Personal Application*

Would you or your spouse like to sometimes spend more time talking before you make love? If so, when and where would you like to talk? In bed? In the living room? Over a cup of coffee in the kitchen?

Do either of you think you sometimes talk too much before making love? If so, write any changes you think you should make, if any.

Make Love in Private

Making love should be a private experience between you and your spouse. Take the steps necessary to be far from other people's eyes and ears.

Make your bedroom a sanctuary.

Make your bedroom a sanctuary for the two of you throughout the day, not just when you make love. Train your children to knock and then wait for permission before they open the door or enter the room. If there is a chance children will walk in when you make love, put a lock on your door and use it when you are sexually intimate.

If noise travels in your house, play background music or wait until the children go to sleep. Be aware that sound can travel through heating ducts. As a young man, I didn't know this. Our bedroom was on the opposite side of the house from the children, so we imagined they couldn't hear us. One day, one of our sons told me, "Dad, I think you should know that we can hear you through the heating vent." I thanked him for the information and plugged the vent.

If you have older children who stay up late, when you retire to your room say, "We want some private time now, so please don't disturb us or call us to the phone." Do this regularly to have quiet times to talk or read, not just when you make love. Another idea for older kids would be to send them out to eat dinner or watch a movie when you wish to be alone.

Don't seek a thrill by making love in public places.

Don't try to "get away" with making love in public or semi-public places where you might get caught. Sex should be an expression of love. Seeking the artificial excitement of wondering if others will see you has nothing to do with love. Although it can be pleasant to make love outside (Song of Songs 1:16), be sure you are private.

 *Personal Application*

Do you need to be more careful to make love in private or to avoid interruptions? ❑ Yes ❑ No

What are the problems?

What changes will you make?

Putting It All Together

Key point: Approach making love with sensitivity. Be available.

●

Memory verse: *"Come away, my lover" (Song of Songs 8:14).*

 *Action Plan*

Choose one or two things from this chapter to work on this week.

1.

2.

Chapter 6

Give Each Other Pleasure

Let my lover come into his garden and taste
its choice fruits (Song of Songs 4:16).

Sexual intimacy consists of two things: expressing love and receiving love. The most important of these by far is expressing love. As Jesus taught us, *"It is more blessed to give than to receive" (Acts 20:35).* This principle applies to every aspect of your life, including sex.

As you read this chapter, you will find ways in which you can more perfectly show love to your mate. And you will discover ways to enjoy his or her love more and more. Pray as you read. Ask God to help your lovemaking be thrilling for both of you.

Seek to Please Your Spouse

Mark seemed like an ideal Christian. He led hundreds of people to the Lord. He volunteered much time to his church and other ministries. He seemed to be a totally generous person whose only desire was to serve others. Yet when in bed with his wife Wendy, his only thought was to enjoy himself. Once he had an orgasm, he was finished. He never considered Wendy's desires.

It took a surprisingly large number of counseling sessions before Mark grasped how self-centered he had been. When he realized his selfishness and lack of love, he felt a deep sense of shame and regret. He began to rebuild his sexual relationship with his wife, basing it on serving her.

As he did this, he was surprised to find that the more he showed love to his wife, the better he felt and the more he enjoyed their times of sexual intimacy. He learned the truth of Jesus' words, *"It is more blessed to give than to receive" (Acts 20:35).*

Consider Craig, another person with the wrong attitude. He was upset because Gail, his wife, never wanted to make love. When I asked her why, she said he got drunk and the smell of alcohol on his breath made her sick. She added that he drank so much he was often unable to come to a climax, making sex an almost unbearable ordeal.

Craig obviously had the wrong attitude. Instead of complaining, he needed to be sensitive to what Gail was saying and seek to please and serve her—not to mention overcoming his drunkenness.

Express love.

Don't assume your husband or wife feels loved simply because you are making love. Say things like, "I love you" and "I'm so glad to be married to you." Minister to your mate emotionally, not just physically.

 *Personal Application*

What can you say or do to convey an unmistakable message of love to your spouse?

Learn what your spouse enjoys.

Gary looked embarrassed but seemed eager to learn. He, his wife Cynthia and I were discussing their sexual relationship and Cynthia had just said that she never had an orgasm when they made love. Gary always finished quickly and left her frustrated, on the threshold.

As we talked about ways he could give her pleasure, I asked if he ever stimulated her clitoris. He sheepishly said he didn't know where it was. When I asked if she would mind showing him later that evening, she smiled and said she would be glad to.

Gary turned out to be an eager student and quickly learned how to give Cynthia pleasure. The next week, in my office, both glowed as they talked about their newfound passion.

When making love, instead of concentrating on what you would enjoy, focus on what would please your spouse. Ask what he or she finds romantic and enjoyable. Learn about likes and dislikes when it comes to touching, holding, squeezing, kissing and nibbling. Don't assume that what gives you pleasure also gives your spouse pleasure.

Read Christian books about sex and romance, but realize that your mate's desires may not be what the books say. There are lots of differences between people. Every time you read, "men like this" or "women like that," be aware that there are exceptions.

Listen to your spouse. Don't be like Jim, a man who didn't believe his wife Bonnie when she asked him not to do certain things as they made love. He responded by saying, "I know you love it, because you always have an orgasm," and refused to stop. He didn't understand that although her body responded, she really wanted him to stop. She was like someone who does not like being tickled. Although she laughs, the laughter is misleading. It is not a happy laughter. Instead, it is a helpless, frustrated, angry laughter.

Personal Application

What sexual activities does your spouse enjoy? (If you haven't talked about this recently, ask.)

Take enough time when you make love.

Many couples rush through making love. As a result, they often miss out on the emotional closeness they might have enjoyed, and the wife (or husband) may not have an orgasm.

Don't be in a hurry to begin intercourse. Foreplay, the time before the husband sexually enters the wife, is important both emotionally and for physical stimulation. Take your time. Enjoy the intimacy of being close and allow the sense of excitement to build.

There is not, of course, a "correct" length of time to make love. Sometimes both of you will want to take a long time. Other times, both may want to move forward more quickly. The key is to take long enough for each one to feel satisfied.

✎ *Personal Application*

Do you like the amount of time you usually take when making love? ❑ Yes ❑ No

Ask your spouse the same question. What changes would either of you like to see?

_____

Make love enthusiastically.

Although he wrote in a different context, Paul illustrated an important principle when he wrote, *"Whatever you do, work at it with all your heart" (Colossians 3:23).* Let this principle of enthusiastic participation guide you in everything you do, including making love. Even if you do not feel like being sexually intimate, throw yourself into it with a willing heart. When you do, there's a good chance you'll discover real enthusiasm growing in you.

There may be times, however, when you are tired or not in the mood to be passionate, yet you agree to be sexually intimate to demonstrate love. At these times, be as involved as possible, but don't feel guilty if you lack extreme enthusiasm.

 *Personal Application*

Do you make love enthusiastically? ❏ Yes ❏ No

If your answer is "no," write a prayer asking God's help.

Do not be angry if your mate seems unenthusiastic.

If your spouse it not passionate when you make love, it's possible that his or her lack of enthusiasm stems from your inconsiderate words or actions. Ask yourself:

- Are there any ways in which I have not been a good friend to my spouse?

- Was my timing bad? Did I want to make love late at night or when my mate was exhausted, stressed or sick?

- Could I have helped more with the kids and household chores in the hours before we made love?

- Was I selfish as we made love?

Although your mate's lack of passion could be related to your inconsiderateness, it could come from many other causes. Perhaps your spouse is uncomfortable with making love. Maybe he or she simply is tired.

Whatever the reason, if your spouse is willing to make love, yet doesn't seem passionate, avoid responding with hurt feelings or resentment. Instead, look upon his or her willingness as a gift of love.

 *Personal Application*

Are you sometimes upset because your spouse does not seem enthusiastic when you make love?
❑ Yes ❑ No

If so, how will you respond in the future?

Seek to bring your spouse to a climax.

Make it a goal to give your spouse an exhilarating experience that culminates with an orgasm. Do not be self-centered, simply seeking to satisfy your own desires.

Husbands

Two key themes to increasing your wife's pleasure are to (1) have a loving relationship with her all the time, not just before times of sexual intimacy and (2) stimulate her clitoris when you make love. The following guidelines expand upon these points and add a few more:

- **Be friendly and respectful throughout the day.**

  As I have stressed throughout this book, your overall relationship has a profound impact upon your wife's feelings about sex. Talk throughout the day. Show her you respect, approve of and love her.

- **Be gentle as you make love.**

  Let her know that you are expressing love, not just having a sexual experience.

- **Start with non-sexual hugs and touches.**

  Foreplay is especially important for your wife's arousal. Don't rush through it. She is likely to enjoy making love much more if you start by hugging and caressing her without focusing on her breasts and vagina. As time goes on, slowly change to touches that are more sexual in nature.

- **Stimulate her by gently caressing her clitoris.**

  Fondling her clitoris has an effect similar to what you experience when she massages your penis. Some commentators say this is the action described in Song of Songs 2:6 and 8:3, stating that the proper translation should be that the man's right hand "fondles" or "sexually stimulates" his wife, not that his right arm "embraces" her.

Gently caress her clitoris during foreplay. Once you enter her, your penis will maintain pressure on it. In addition, if she would like it, continue to caress her clitoris with your fingers after entering her.

- **Do not begin intercourse until she is ready.**

Wait to enter her sexually until she desires you to do so. If you are uncertain about when is a good time, ask her to say when she is ready.

If you have trouble delaying your orgasm, ask her not to touch your penis when your excitement level builds too high.

- **Try to delay climaxing until she has an orgasm.**

Once you begin intercourse, try to postpone your orgasm until she has one, since hers depends a great deal upon feeling your erect penis against her clitoris. It may take self-control, but the results are worth it for both of you. You will have an extended time of ex-cited anticipation, and she will be much more likely to experience an orgasm.

- **If you have an orgasm first, bring her to a climax.**

If you ejaculate before she has an orgasm, and if your wife would like it, continue to stimulate her clitoris with your fingers until she, too, has an or-gasm. If she asks you to stop, follow her wishes.

Personal Application

Husbands, which of the above points will you work on to increase your wife's enjoyment?

_____

Wives

You can make your spouse's experience much more exciting and help bring him to a climax. Your active participation in making love is the key.

- **Strengthen and use your PC muscle.**

  Do Kegal exercises to develop the pubococcygeus (PC) muscle. This will help you put a firm, squeezing pressure upon your husband's penis while it is in your vagina, providing greater sexual pleasure for him, as well as for yourself.

- **Be passionate.**

  Peggy described passively lying in bed as her husband made love to her, her thoughts ones of frustration and impatience as she waited for him to hurry up and get it over with. She had told him to make it fast and was upset that he was taking so long to come to a climax. She had no idea that her negative attitude and inactivity were a big part of the problem.

Most men are highly aroused when their wife makes love with enthusiasm. The more passion you display, the greater his excitement will be.

- **Talk to him.**

   You will greatly increase your husband's excitement, and probably yours, if you express words and sounds of pleasure, praise and appreciation as you make love.

- **Be sensitive as your husband grows older.**

   As your husband grows older, he may take longer before he is sufficiently aroused to begin intercourse. Ask what he would like you to do to build up his excitement. As you engage in foreplay, fondle and caress his penis until he is ready to enter you. It may be appropriate to switch roles: Instead of telling him when you are ready, ask him to say when he is ready and then let him know if you are, too.

 *Personal Application*

Wives, which of these activities will you work on to increase your husband's enjoyment?

Don't think you must have a simultaneous orgasm.

Some couples think they've failed if they do not have a simultaneous orgasm. They haven't failed at all. Although a simultaneous orgasm can be exhilarating, it also can be exhilarating if first one has an orgasm, then the other. There's no "right" pattern. In fact, if the wife has a longer orgasm than her husband, which is often the case, she might enjoy it more if she has hers first.

Do not worry if either fails to have an orgasm.

There may be times when you or your spouse do not reach a climax due to health problems, tiredness, tension, worry or other reasons. There's no need to be thrown by this or think you have failed. It happens now and then even in the best marriages. Worrying about it is likely to make you more self-conscious the next time you make love. Ask God for wisdom, patience and a sense of humor.

Husbands, although you should give your wife as much pleasure as possible, do not insist on her having an orgasm or multiple orgasms. Follow her lead. You have not "failed" unless you made love selfishly and did not try to give her pleasure. You will not get a trophy for being pushy or demanding she have an orgasm. You will get a trophy for being kind, gentle, loving and responsive to her wishes.

Wives, if your husband does not ejaculate, he may feel like a failure. Reassure him that it's okay and you're sure he will have an orgasm in the future. Let him know you enjoyed being intimate and are looking forward to the next time.

 *Personal Application*

Have you sometimes felt like a failure if you or your spouse did not have an orgasm? ❏ Yes ❏ No

How will you respond in the future if this happens again?

Do Not Make Love with a Fantasy

Many people engage in mental fantasies to increase their sexual stimulation. If you do this, you may think about pornographic images or visualize another person as you make love. Or you may think about things you wish your spouse would do but is not willing to do.

Don't do this! Fantasizing changes your times of sexual intimacy from experiences of truly giving and receiving love, of connecting emotionally and physically, into times of using the other person for sexual gratification.

Teresa, a woman I counseled, illustrated this when she said, "In all the times we've had sex, I never made love to my husband. I always imagined he was another man."

You may be like Teresa, choosing to entertain fantasies as you make love. Or perhaps you don't want to fantasize, yet as you make love, you find yourself remembering sexual experiences with other people or images from pornography. In either case, these thoughts corrupt your sexual experiences. Instead of connecting emotionally with your mate, you disconnect.

If what you fantasize is sinful, you displease God. You also cheat your spouse and yourself. If you catch the vision of truly loving your mate when you make love, not just engaging in sexual activity, you will experience a sense of excitement and exhilaration that you never could have imagined.

Practice the following guidelines to begin to experience God's freedom. These are good ideas even if you do not have trouble fantasizing.

- Pray about the problem. Ask the Lord to cleanse your mind and help you truly love your spouse.

- Pray for God's blessing before you make love.

- As you make love, concentrate on loving your spouse. Think about him or her.

- Keep your eyes open as you make love and look at your mate. (This is not an absolute law; it is simply a technique to focus on your spouse.)

- Talk with your spouse as you make love. Focus your attention on him or her. Say such words as "I love you," "that feels nice" and "thank you."

Am I suggesting that all fantasies are bad? No. If you and your spouse want to imagine you're on a cruise ship or under a palm tree on a desert island, that's fine. Just don't fantasize that you're making love with someone else, raping your mate or engaging in any other sexual sin.

✎ *Personal Application*

Do you need to focus on loving your spouse instead of fantasizing? ❏ Yes ❏ No

Which of the above guidelines will you practice?

Enjoy Yourself

Sometimes, for one reason or another, a person can't seem to enjoy making love. This can become quite a problem, with the spouse who doesn't enjoy sex trying to get out of it, leaving his or her mate frustrated. At times, the one who doesn't like sex feels guilty for not taking pleasure in what everyone says is a special gift from God.

This lack of enjoyment sometimes comes from a sneaking suspicion that there is something sinful about sex. Sex within marriage gets tainted with the sin of sex outside marriage. Even if someone can see that sex is approved scripturally, it seems wrong, entirely of the flesh, not at all of the spirit.

If this describes you, re-read Chapter 1 to reassure yourself of God's hearty approval of marital lovemaking. As you read, you will see that both the man and woman enthusiastically enjoy sexual intimacy. He exclaims, *"How delightful is your love"* *(Song of Songs 4:10),* and she is thrilled as he *"browses among the lilies" (Song of Songs 2:16).* Making love is God's plan. It is spiritual, not unspiritual.

As I wrote in Chapter 5, even if your friendship has been rocky, or your mate doesn't approach you romantically, you can respond by ministering love to him or her. When you do this, you aren't "prostituting" yourself. Rather, you are reaching out in love to build a bridge between the two of you. As you build this bridge, allow yourself to enjoy the pleasure of being sexually intimate.

Memorize a few verses from Chapter 1 that speak of the pleasure of lovemaking. Ask God to give you a sense of delight in your sexual relationship similar to that experienced by the lover and his beloved in the Song of Songs. Also pray to enjoy touching and being touched. With God's help, you will discover that you can truly enjoy yourself.

 *Personal Application*

Do you allow yourself to enjoy making love?
❏ Yes   ❏ No

Talk to God: *"Lord, thank you for the gift of sex. Please help me to fully grasp that it is holy and good within my marriage. Help me to freely enjoy myself the next time we make love, in Jesus' name."*

Communicate While You Make Love

A couple can be completely silent and enjoy making love. However, something is added when you talk and whisper sweet words. If your spouse is quiet while you make love, it's okay to ask him or her to communicate, but don't pressure him or her to do so.

Some ways to communicate while making love are:

Tell your mate of your love.

Remember, expressing love is at the heart of sexual intimacy.

Express appreciation.

Say that you enjoy what your spouse is doing. Compliment specific features of your spouse's lovemaking, such as her passion or his tenderness. Praise his or her attractiveness.

Make a request.

Feel free to request that your husband or wife do something you desire, such as touch or kiss a certain way. However, don't slip into hurt feelings if your mate doesn't do what you request. Put most of your attention into giving your mate pleasure, not on your desires.

Tell your mate if something bothers or hurts you.

Let your spouse know if something he or she does hurts or bothers you. Speak gently.

Be expressive nonverbally.

As your excitement builds, nonverbal exclamations (that are not *too* loud) can increase your enjoyment and stimulate your spouse. The connection between you becomes a little closer and the opportunity for intimacy is increased.

Personal Application

Do you communicate when making love?
❏ Yes   ❏ No

If not, write one friendly thing you will say the next time you make love.

Enjoy Freedom and Creativity

The Scriptures indicate a great deal of freedom in the sexual activities and positions that a husband and wife may enjoy. The Song of Songs, particularly, paints a rich, sensuous picture, one in which both husband and wife thoroughly enjoy themselves. The language is poetic and leaves much to the reader's imagination, but it is clear that King Solomon and his bride felt free to be creative as they made love.

One or both of you may desire some variety in the time of day that you make love, as well as in activities, positions or locations. There is nothing wrong with that, provided that neither of you falls into a pornographic mentality or tries to force the other into doing something he or she finds uncomfortable.

There also is nothing wrong if both of you are content to continue doing things just as you have in the past.

What sexual activities are permissible?

In general, the Bible does not describe right and wrong sexual activities for a married couple. Instead, its imagery leaves much room for creativity and mutual exploration.

Some people enter marriage not understanding the freedom a couple can enjoy. I remember one woman who refused to let her husband see her naked. She insisted on making love in the dark.

Another woman thought it was immoral for her husband to touch her breasts. She needed to study Solomon's words: *"Your stature is like that of the palm, and your breasts like clusters of fruit. I said, 'I will climb the palm tree; I will take hold of its fruit'" (Song of Songs 7:7-8).* Proverbs 5:19 talks about the same thing.

Although Solomon wrote about the husband enjoying holding his wife's breasts, most biblical passages describing sexual intimacy leave the details to the reader's imagination. For example:

 Let my lover come into his garden and taste its choice fruits (Song of Songs 4:16).

My lover has gone down to his garden, to the beds of spices, to browse in the gardens and to gather lilies. I am my lover's and my lover is mine; he browses among the lilies (Song of Songs 6:2-3).

Notice that God used metaphors instead of spelling it out. Instead of explicitly describing their lovemaking, or saying exactly where the husband "browsed," he painted a picture of delightful, uninhibited enjoyment. The commentary accompanying the New International Version Study Bible says, "The lover, enjoying intimacies with the beloved, is compared to a graceful gazelle nibbling from lily to lily in undisturbed enjoyment of exotic delicacies."

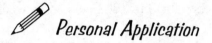

Personal Application

What has been your attitude toward expressing freedom or creativity in your sexual relationship?

Be guided by godly principles.

Although God does not list every activity that a married couple may or may not engage in, his Word gives us principles to apply. Follow these guidelines as you consider how to enjoy freedom and creativity:

- **Follow biblical commands and principles.**

    Do not disobey God's commands. For example, do not engage in sexual activities with anyone other than your spouse.

- **Focus on expressing love.**

   It is possible to get so caught up in what you want to *do* that you stop expressing *love* to your spouse. If you are not careful, the marriage bed can become a place of tension and anger. Always seek to express love.

- **Do not be ruled by pornographic images.**

   Have you been exposed to pornography? If so, you may have brought unhealthy attitudes into your sexual relationship. Any pornographic images in your mind are not those of people expressing love one to another; they are images of people who do not know how to love. Pray to be free from the effects of pornography.

- **Do not engage in sinful fantasies.**

   Do not act out a rape scene, pretend you are torturing your spouse or imagine you are having sex with someone else. The marriage bed is pure (Hebrews 13:4). Keep it that way.

- **Do not violate either one's conscience or morals.**

   Do not insist on doing something if your spouse thinks it is wrong. As Paul wrote, *"Everything that does not come from faith is sin" (Romans 14:23).*

 *Personal Application*

Do you need to change your attitude or actions based on the above principles? ❑ Yes ❑ No

If you answered "yes," which principles do you want to remember the next time you make love?

_____

Bring up new ideas tenderly.

Although your principal goal should be to give your spouse pleasure, it's okay to talk about your own desires, likes and dislikes, if you do so in a pleasant, non-demanding manner.

Each of you should look not only to your own interests, but also to the interests of others (Philippians 2:4).

Bring up new ideas as a friend. Convey the message that you are not criticizing your spouse and that you are not saying you don't already enjoy making love.

✏ *Personal Application*

Have you approached your spouse about new ideas in a friendly manner? ❑ Yes ❑ No

If not, how should you bring them up?

_____

Respond to new ideas lovingly.

Don't be angry or insulted, or feel that you have been displeasing, if your spouse wants to try something different.

Imagine that you ate spaghetti for dinner every night and that it was prepared the same way each time. After a few years, you might still love spaghetti, and you might appreciate the cook's skill, but you might wish to add some new spices or eat something else now and then for variety. If that were the case, there would be no reason for the cook to feel insulted.

Likewise, there's no reason for you to be upset if your spouse expresses a desire to do something different in your sexual relationship. Do not think less of him or her for suggesting playing background music, making love with the wife on top or any of countless other possible variations in your normal routine.

As I wrote earlier, the Bible allows a great deal of freedom and creativity in the sexual activities that a husband and wife may enjoy. Seek to discover ways to express love to your spouse by "stretching" a little. Read the Song of Songs and ask God to help you experience more freedom. Learn to grow, together, in ways of expressing and receiving love. Although you may feel awkward at first, seek to give your spouse pleasure and allow yourself to enjoy being creative in your sexual experience.

If you say "no," say it courteously.

Joyce was upset because her husband Frank said he would like to engage in oral sex with her. Although he didn't pressure her, she said he must be perverted to have such desires.

I pointed out that the Bible does not say anything about a husband and wife engaging in oral sex. Since the Bible encourages sexual freedom within marriage, it would be wrong to call her husband's desires sinful or perverted. I added that the key point was that he didn't pressure her.

As we talked, Joyce regained respect for her husband. Although she still felt uncomfortable with oral sex, she was able to say "no" in a loving and respectful manner.

If your spouse suggests doing something that is not sinful, but is beyond your comfort level, don't violate your conscience. You could say something such as, "I'm not comfortable with that. I'll pray about it, but for now I hope you will respect me by not pressuring me." Over time, as you pray and study the Bible, the Lord may give you new freedom in some areas. In the meantime, follow your conscience.

If your spouse brings up a suggestion that is obviously sinful, such as watching pornography or engaging in sex with others, speak courteously, yet take a firm stand. Always obey the Word of God.

Even at a time like this, watch your attitude. Instead of condemning your mate, pray for him or her. If your spouse continues to pressure you to do things that are offensive, continue to refuse and suggest that you both see your pastor or a biblical counselor.

 *Personal Application*

How do you respond when your spouse suggests doing something new sexually?

Write any changes you will make in how you respond.

Be gracious if your mate says "no" to your ideas.

If your spouse doesn't feel like doing something you suggest, demonstrate your love by respecting those wishes. Avoid becoming bitter and don't try to force your desires on him or her.

You can enjoy your sexual relationship without doing everything you would like. If you have to give up a specific dream, it is a small sacrifice compared to the sacrifice Christ made on the cross for you.

As I wrote earlier, examine your motives or desires. Be careful not to get caught up in performance or try to realize some sort of pornographic dream. Many men enter marriage with ungodly attitudes about sex and think the only problem in their sex life is that their wife is inhibited. Such men usually are unaware that they aren't expressing love to their wives.

For example, if a man looks upon sex as a means of conquest, this can carry over into his marriage. He may compulsively pressure his wife to do more, acting as he did with girlfriends whom he pressured to "go a little further."

If your spouse does not make love with the creativity you desire, it is possible he or she is reacting to deficits in your overall relationship. Review Chapter 2 to see if you have contributed to the problem.

It is possible, of course, that you have been courteous, respectful and loving, yet your spouse is still extremely inhibited. I know of families in which one person absolutely refused to make love. In an extreme situation such as this, see a pastor or biblical counselor for help.

 *Personal Application*

Have you pressured your spouse to do things he or she did not want to do?   ❑ Yes   ❑ No

Write a prayer asking God to help you be patient, loving and forbearing in the future.

Be Romantic After Making Love

Continue to be friendly and romantic after you make love. Talk for a while, expressing love. Don't be like Harold, a man who scored his wife Millie on a scale of one to ten after they made love. He sprinkled in specific criticisms and ways for her to improve. It's easy to understand why Millie lost interest in being sexually intimate with him.

 *Personal Application*

Think about the way you act after making love. Are there any changes you should make? ❑ Yes ❑ No

If so, write them here.

Talk about Sexual Problems

Sex is one of the most sensitive areas a couple can talk about. However, despite the discomfort, it is important to talk about desires, frustrations, problems, medical issues, job pressures, impotence, menopause or other issues that affect your sexual relationship.

Timing is important. It's usually better not to bring up problems right before or after making love. Consider saving your comments until the next day.

Talk as friends. For example, if the husband does not achieve or maintain an erection, he shouldn't blame his wife. And she shouldn't be angry at him or consider him a failure.

If you think your spouse has a sexual problem, be willing to talk about your part. Avoid simply saying, "You've got a problem."

If either of you is not interested in making love, review this book together to see if you can identify possible causes and solutions. Get a medical checkup. See a biblical counselor. Take whatever steps are necessary to improve this vital aspect of marriage.

 *Personal Application*

Do you and your spouse need to talk about your sexual relationship? ❏ Yes ❏ No

If your answer is "yes," what do you need to discuss?

Write a plan describing when and how you will approach your spouse.

Be Patient and Understanding

It can take time, thought and effort to develop a rewarding sexual relationship. There may be awkward, embarrassing or unsuccessful moments. When there are, try to be sensitive and keep a sense of humor. As you grow together in love and wisdom, you will also grow together as lovers.

If you have been unavailable to make love because you are sick, and your spouse seems sexually frustrated, ask God to help you be understanding instead of resentful or guilty.

If your spouse is sexually unavailable because of illness or other reasons, seek God's help to be patient and help your mate. Do not say you can hardly wait to make love since this may cause him or her to feel guilty or resentful.

See this as a time to focus on your relationship with God. Enjoy the satisfaction that comes from a closer walk with him.

Also be understanding if your spouse has had bad experiences or poor teachings about sex. It may be difficult for him or her to recover from these hurts or misconceptions.

 *Personal Application*

Do you need to be more patient and understanding with your spouse? ❑ Yes ❑ No

In what ways will you demonstrate greater patience?

Last Thoughts

I'd like to close this chapter by reminding you to never forget what is at the heart of sexual intimacy: giving and receiving love. When you focus on loving, not performance, you will find your love burning like a mighty flame. Over the years, your passion will become more and more exhilarating.

 Place me like a seal over your heart, like a seal on your arm; for love is as strong as death, its jealousy unyielding as the grave. It burns like blazing fire, like a mighty flame. Many waters cannot quench love; rivers cannot wash it away. If one were to give all the wealth of his house for love, it would be utterly scorned (Song of Songs 8:6-7).

Putting It All Together

Key point: Focus on giving your spouse pleasure. Learn to express and receive love in your sexual union, not simply "have sex."

•

Memory verse: *"Let my lover come into his garden and taste its choice fruits" (Song of Songs 4:16).*

 *Action Plan*

Choose one or two things from this chapter to work on this week.

1.

2.

My Plan

Now that you have finished reading this book, take a few minutes to review each chapter, particularly the "Putting It All Together" section at the end of each chapter. Choose from one to three things to work on in the coming month and write them on this page.

1.

2.

3.

Looking Ahead

If you have not studied the previous seven books in this series, let me encourage you to read them. They will help you develop an intimate and lasting friendship that will enrich your sex life.

After you read all eight books, consider encouraging friends to study this series in a small-group setting. By sharing what you have learned and inviting others to study, you can make a big difference in people's lives.

When you talk with other couples, let them know this material isn't just for people who have problems—it's also for those who want to make a great marriage even better.

Step out and be a blessing to others! If the eight books in the *Marriage by the Book* series and the *Group Leaders' Guide* are not available in your church or bookstore, write to BibleSource Publications for how-to-order information. Mailing and e-mail addresses are on the inside front page of this book.

May God richly bless you as you grow in your marriage and as you share with others.

Doug Britton

More Resources

Author, speaker and marriage and family counselor Doug Britton has helped thousands of people since entering the counseling field in 1967. His ministry focuses on showing how to apply the Word of God to daily life in insightful, practical ways.

Online Daily-Living Bible Studies

Visit www.DougBrittonBooks.com to read and print free online Bible studies on marriage, parenting, depression, jealousy, self-concept, temptation, anger and other daily-living topics.

While at the site, sign up to receive one or two emails each month announcing new online studies, as well as news about new books, seminars and retreats with Doug Britton.

Seminars and Retreats

Doug teaches on a wide variety of topics at seminars and retreats. Subject matter includes marriage, parenting, biblical counseling, depression, jealousy and insecurity, self-concept, finances, temptation and anger. For information about sponsoring a seminar or retreat at your church or community center, go to www.DougBrittonBooks.com.

See next page for more resources

Practical Books for Daily Living

Learn how to apply the Bible's truths in all areas of your life. If the following books by Doug Britton are not available at your local bookstore, you can purchase them online at www.DougBrittonBooks.com.

- **Conquering Depression:** A Journey Out of Darkness into God's Light
- **Defeating Temptation:** Biblical Secrets to Self-Control
- **Getting Started:** Taking New Steps in My Walk with Jesus
- **Healing Life's Hurts:** God's Solutions When Others Wound You
- **Overcoming Jealousy and Insecurity:** Biblical Steps to Living without Fear
- **Self-Concept:** Understanding Who You are in Christ
- **Strengthening Your Marriage:** 12 Exercises for Married Couples
- **Successful Christian Parenting:** Nurturing with Insight and Disciplining in Love
- **Victory over Grumpiness, Irritation and Anger**

Marriage by the Book (eight-book series)
- **Book 1 – Laying a Solid Foundation**
- **Book 2 – Making Christ the Cornerstone**
- **Book 3 – Encouraging Your Spouse**
- **Book 4 – Extending Grace to Your Mate**
- **Book 5 – Talking with Respect and Love**
- **Book 6 – Improving Your Teamwork**
- **Book 7 – Putting Money in its Place**
- **Book 8 – Fanning the Flames of Romance**
- **Marriage by the Book Group Leaders' Guide**